D1713292

Tales From Behind the Lights

A Glimpse at 40 Years Behind the Scenes During the "Second Golden Age of Movies"

By Paul Caven

DEDICATION

I dedicate this memoir to my beautiful, loving, and understanding wife Denise, the best "crew wife" ever! Her unconditional love and support helped me endure the long lonely nights away from home. Her encouragement inspired me to put pen to paper here.

I also dedicate this to my sweet daughter Danielle, a heavenly angel with broken wings who every day must learn to fly. Someday she too will have perfect wings. Danielle has taught me humility and perseverance in the realization that no matter what cards fate deals you, your quality of life is determined by your own attitude and willpower, and she has an abundance of both!

ACKNOWLEDGEMENTS

I especially want to thank my wife Denise for her immeasurable assistance in writing this book. Because she was with me on many locations, she remembered several things that I had forgotten.

A heartfelt thank you to Richmond "Aggie" Aguilar for bringing me along on his magical mystery tour. Aggie was my Boss, my Mentor and is still my best friend.

I also want to thank and acknowledge the following people for their important contribution to this work:

My wonderful niece Moira Giammatteo, my favorite proofreader.

My high school friend Dennis Tonsing for his frank and objective edit... thanks for the tough love.

Our long-time friend, Shelley Stump, for her comprehensive final edit. Without her immeasurable assistance this project would never have been completed.

Tammy Gay for the thorough final proofread. Thanks for grading my paper.

IMDb.com for refreshing my memory on some of the details I may have forgotten.

TABLE OF CONTENTS

PREFACE

I am writing this book as a personal memoir of my career in TV and the movies. It is primarily a walk down memory lane, but it is also an opportunity for me to share some of my experience and insights about the joys, challenges, and technical lighting changes I experienced over a 40 year career in "lighting" that spanned five decades. I hope my stories will provide a little more "history" of the TV and movies in which I had the privilege to creatively participate over many decades.

I begin in this Preface with a general overview of the history of the film industry to set the context for the personal stories and photos I share in this book. This description of the film industry is in my own words and may/may not comport with others' understanding or opinions.

Following this general history, the remainder of the book chronicles my experience and career in TV and the "Movies" with information about how the art of film lighting evolved over the five decades I had the wonderful opportunity to work in the industry. These writings chronicle my personal experiences and present opinions that I formed from my encounters. No opinions are intended to cause difficulty for anyone, they are just my memories and opinions.

My Short History of the Magic of Film Making

The Major Film Studios. The "First Golden Age of the Movies" was the 1930s and 1940s. Those great movies and wonderful musicals helped the country through The Great Depression, and The Second World War. All those movies were produced by major studios.

The studios were run by studio heads or owners like Jack Warner, Samuel Goldwyn, Louie B. Mayer, and Walt Disney, and the studio heads controlled the entire industry. They owned the actors under contract to them. They had writers and directors under contract. They had all the departments staffed and equipped. They had their own cameras and film lab, their own lights and generators, a full construction mill to build all the sets, and a machine shop where they could fabricate anything you wanted. Each studio hired thousands of people.

The problem was by the 1970s and 1980s the studio heads were all gone, replaced by boards of directors and lawyers who were more interested in widening the distribution of films than making them. They failed to update any of their equipment. Their cameras became outdated; their lights became unusable; technology passed them by. Say what you will about the old studio heads, they were tyrannical and oppressive but they knew the business and they knew how to make good movies.

The Transition to Independent Film Making. The slow death of the old studio system gave birth to the independent producer in the 1960s and 1970s and to what was later called "The Second Golden Age of Movies." Independent producers were able to secure their own financing and film their movies without interference from the studio. *Easy Rider* is a perfect example. That was filmed on a very low budget, non-union, by an independent producer.

Easy Rider was a very powerful film, but the independent producers did not have a good way to distribute the film. The studios still had all the distribution outlets locked-up, so, the producers still had to dance with the major studios. They struck a deal with Columbia Studios to distribute it for a percentage of the profit. It made hundreds of millions of dollars, and became a cult classic.

This success inspired other independent producers. If they could get the studios to just distribute their film, without them interfering in the production, they could increase their profits tenfold. What followed was a flood of low budget non-union films, but the quality was poor. The labor pool for low budget non-union films was thin. So, independent producers decided to increase their budgets and pay people more than the studios in an effort to lure the best union people away from the studio. For the first time, independent producers were able to make high quality films that the studios wanted to release.

I benefitted personally from this shift to independent productions. I had the great fortune of getting hooked up with one of the premiere independent cinematographers, Laszlo Kovacs and his legendary gaffer

Richmond "Aggie" Aguilar. Laszlo and Aggie worked on *Easy Rider*. I worked with them on many independent films like *King of Marvin Gardens* and *Paper Moon*.

Changes I Witnessed in the Art of Lighting. Because of the span of my career, I had the opportunity to witness monumental changes in the lighting aspect of the industry. Arguably many of these changes happened first in the commercial field, and then spread throughout the industry.

Commercial gaffers started using a new type of movie light, the Hydrargyrum Medium-Arc Iodide (HMI), which is the type of bulb it uses. The HMI had several advantages particularly for the commercial field because it produces high light output for low wattage. That meant when we were filming in someone's kitchen, we were able to plug our lights into the wall outlets without tripping breakers.

That worked fine for small commercial productions but not so well for TV or movie productions and was a disaster for the studios. First, the only units the manufacturer had made thus far were too small; they worked well for lighting in a kitchen but not so well for lighting a big ballroom. So, they started making bigger and bigger HMI lights.

HMI lights are great lights and still are widely used today. But, the major problem was that they only work on AC current. From day one the studios had always used DC current exclusively. Their stages and back lot were all wired with DC current. Mainly because the huge arc lamps used DC only and they were the workhorse of the whole industry. We had no experience with AC power and knew very little about it.

The more popular HMIs became, the more it became evident that our cabling systems were going to have to change. DC power does not need to be grounded; it only needs two wires, a positive and a negative, but no ground wire. AC power has to be grounded, which requires an extra wire. This meant that not only did all our cable systems need to change but also our lights. The plugs for our lights were all two wire DC, ungrounded plugs.

For the next several years, in the mid 1980s, different manufacturers scrambled to come up with an approved system. In the meantime, we had to try to adapt as best we could. Unfortunately some people got hurt and one of our members even got electrocuted on the set. Eventually, a couple of approved systems were devised and all the studios and all the independent equipment vendors had to buy all new cable systems; they also had to acquire a full cadre of new HMI lights and all the lighting crew personnel had to be retrained. It was a monumental change, indeed, that happened gradually over time until Underwriters Laboratory (UL) approved some of the new systems. The changeover was complete within about five years.

After the change from DC current to AC current, a whole new world of opportunity opened up for lighting equipment. Along with HMI lights, we were able to use a brand-new type of florescent light. A company called KYNO FLO invented and marketed a line of florescent lamps, AC only, made for lighting film productions. The switchover also allowed us to start using some of the AC-only dimming systems and cabling systems used on stage productions, as well as the dimmer control consoles. This enabled us to control every light from the dimmer board.

Set lighting continues to evolve with new innovations in lighting. Since I retired in 2007, they have begun to use new LED lights and computer-controlled moving lights like they use in rock concerts. They now have a whole new catalog of lights that are AC current only.

Changes in Titles for Lighting Personnel. From the time I entered the industry, I was introduced to the unique titles used in the lighting industry like "gaffer" and "best boy." I describe the meaning of those terms where they first appear in the book. These terms were throwbacks to the earliest days in the movie industry.

My career spanned enough time, however, that I was part of the change in "titles" that occurred in 1992. As part of the negotiation of our new 1992 I.A.T.S.E, Local 728 union contract, they changed our job titles to Chief Lighting Technician, Assistant Chief Lighting Technician and so on. It was kind of a bone-of-contention at the time. The Camera I.A.T.S.E., Local 600 did not want us to have the word "Lighting" in our job title because, they argued, the camera people were technically responsible for the overall look and that included lighting. We talked the producers into doing it because we argued that lighting is what we do… and that is all we do. So, in my career the title "gaffer" changed to "Chief Lighting Technician". The "best boy" title changed to "Assistant Chief Lighting Technician." We fought Goliath and won!

Being Part of the Collaborative Creative Crew of Film Production. Movie making is definitively a collaborative creative endeavor that requires the best work of everyone committed to the project. That was one of the things I found most rewarding in working in the industry. As we know, most of the focus on films, especially when they are formally recognized with awards, etc., is on the Cast, the Director, the Producers, and the Writers. Many of you may remember actors and others at awards shows in their acceptance speeches, thanking all "the crew" that helped make it all happen. This book is my opportunity to highlight the importance of the work of those "behind the camera" in all the productions I had the good fortune to contribute to over the years.

Happy reading!

PAUL CAVEN FILMOGRAPHY

Camelot — 1967
Bonanza — 1971
The FBI — 1972
The Streets of San Francisco - 1972
What's Up Doc - 1971
Deliverance - 1971
The King of Marvin Gardens — 1971-1972
Paper Moon - 1972
Freebie and the Bean - 1973
Huckleberry Finn - 1973
At Long Last Love - 1973
For Pete's Sake - 1973
Doc Savage - 1974
Shampoo - 1974
Baby Blue Marine - 1975
Entertainer - 1975
Harry and Walter Go to New York - 1975
Friendly Persuasion - 1975
Sybil - 1976
Nickelodeon- 1976
One on One - 1976
Murder At the World Series - 1976
Casey's Shadow - 1976
The Cheap Detective - 1977
Hooper - 1978
Every Which Way But Loose - 1978
The Runner Stumbles - 1978
Heart Beat - 1978
The Electric Horseman - 1978
The Baltimore Bullet - 1979
Before and After - 1979
How to Beat the High Cost of Living - 1979
The Postman Always Rings Twice - 1980
Moviola: The Scarlett O'Hara War - 1980
On Golden Pond - 1980
Wrong is Right- 1981
Goliath Awaits - 1981
Frances - 1981
The Toy - 1982
Star 80 - 1982
The Grace Kelly Story - 1982
This Girl for Hire - 1983
Swing Shift - 1983
The Woman in Red - 1983
It Came Upon a Midnight Clear - 1984

Mask - 1984
Quicksilver — 1984-1985
Shadow Chasers - 1984
Legal Eagles - 1986
Nuts - 1986
Little Nikita - 1987
Sunset - 1987
Nerds of a Feather — 1988
Spys' & Lovers/Nerds of a Feather — 1988
Say Anything - 1988
An Innocent Man - 1989
Tango & Cash - 1989
Navy Seals - 1989
Shattered - 1990
Kindergarten Cop - 1990
Radio Flyer - 1990
Sleepwalkers - 1991
Chaplin - 1991
Home Alone 2: Lost in New York - 1992
Sleepless in Seattle - 1992
The Next Karate Kid - 1993
Junior - 1993
Free Willy 2: The Adventure Home - 1994
Copycat - 1994
Father of the Bride II - 1995
Primal Fear - 1995
Multiplicity - 1995
My Fellow Americans - 1996
My Best Friend's Wedding - 1996
As Good As It Gets - 1997
Sphere - 1997
Midnight in the Garden of Good and Evil - 1997
Always Outnumbered - 1997
Rush Hour - 1997
The Out-of-Towners - 1998
Never Been Kissed - 1998
For the Love of the Game - 1999
Action - 1999
JAG - 2003
Dr. Vegas - 2004
Six Feet Under — 2000-2005
Modern Men - 2005
Because I Said So - 2006
Raines - 2006
Tell Me You Love Me - 2006

WHY GROW UP WHEN YOU CAN MAKE MOVIES?

I was born in December of 1946 in Glasgow, Scotland, during the worst snow storm in 100 years, according to my mother. I guess that's why I have always hated cold weather. In 1948, my family moved from snowy Glasgow, to sunny Southern California. We lived for several years in the Echo Park area of Los Angeles, and in 1952 we moved again, to Lima Street in Burbank. Our house on Lima Street was just three blocks north of Warner Brothers Studio.

Some of us kids used to sneak through a hole in the fence into Warner Brothers back lot on the weekends and play on the back-lot sets. One summer day I decided to sneak into the back lot on a weekday. It turned out they were filming the TV show *The Adventures of Rin Tin Tin* there that day. I saw the young star of the show, Lee Aaker, sitting on the grass off to the side of the set. I knew who he was; I was a big fan of the show. He was about my age so I decided to walk up and say hi. We sat and talked for a while. He thought it was great that I had snuck in, so we hit it off. He introduced me to Rin Tin Tin, the star of the show. We played catch until they had to go to work on the set, then I snuck out the same way I snuck in. I am not sure if that is what sparked my interest in wanting to make movies, but, looking back, I remember thinking, "it would sure be fun." Many years later I bought a T-shirt that said, "Why Grow Up When You Can Make Movies?"

The Rookie Years

When I graduated from high school in 1965, my dad, Ambrose "Amby" Caven, was working at Warner Brothers Studio as the timekeeper in the

1

set lighting department. A few years before he had to change careers in midlife from a baker to studio timekeeper. He had been a union journeyman baker all of his adult life. When Weston's Biscuit Company in Burbank, the bakery factory he was the manager of, decided to move to Tacoma, Washington, dad had to choose whether to move to Tacoma or be out of a job.

Ambrose "Amby" Caven (1965)

He chose not to move to Tacoma. His good friend George Lesley worked in the Accounting Department at Warner Brothers Studios and was able to get him a job in the same department. In those days you needed to know someone to get into the studios.

My dad told me about a new industry trainee program starting for lighting technicians. I signed up, and in August of 1966, I got my first call to work at Warner Brothers. The way the training program was set up, you had to have a certain number of hours working in all of the different facets of Set Lighting, from rigging all the cables and lights on the sets, to learning how to wire the set fixtures and wall outlets and doing the on set lighting during filming, including setting up and running the old arc lamps they used to use. After completing my training period, I was able to join the Union in 1968. I worked at all the major studios but my 'home lot' was always Warner Brothers. I worked there more than anyplace else.

One of the first major movies I worked on at Warner Brothers was *Camelot* with Richard Harris and Vanessa Redgrave. I worked on one of the several rigging crews that rigged their huge sets. After we finished rigging all the sets, they let us young bucks work on the filming crew. On one stage was the forest set where Guinevere enters and where Merlin lives. We rigged hundreds of the old arc lamps up high in the catwalks above the set.

When I say old arc lamps, I mean old. These lamps were from the 1930s. They were the work horse of the lighting industry for decades. Every studio had hundreds of them. They use a very old technology. Actually, this is the same technology used in those spotlights they use at premiers (Klieg Lights), as well as in the movie projectors of the day. They ran on DC only and used two "sticks" of carbon, one hooked up to the positive pole and the other hooked up to the negative pole. When you strike them together, they "arc" and create a high intensity flame about 12 inches long. It was the biggest and brightest light available.

Each of the arc lamps required its own operator. If 100 arc lights were used, 100 operators were needed. The arc lamps needed to be monitored to be sure the flame was maintained and to change the carbons when they burned down. Changing the carbons was always a challenge. There was a little hatch on the side of the lamp that had to be opened and the operator had to reach into the hot light with pliers and gloves to loosen the bolts that held the carbons, then replace them with the new carbons. This work usually had to be done as quickly as possible because the production was waiting for the operator to finish so they could roll again. Because of that, it was virtually impossible to perform this task without hitting your forearm on the hot frame around the hatch. Boy that hurt! You could always tell the guys who were arc operators by the "hash marks" on their arms.

The *Camelot* round table set was built on Warner's highest stage, then Stage 7 (years later they changed all the stage numbers). It is over 100 feet high and one of the highest stages in Hollywood. It is so high that they built a bathroom up in the very top catwalks so that people working up there did not have to come all the way down to the floor to use the bathroom. One just had to make sure not to flush during a take. There was also an enormous exterior set of the castle built on the back lot (now office space and parking).

I will never forget the sense of amazement I felt as I stood leaning over the handrails of the catwalks perched high above the set watching with wonder while the lighting gaffer lit the set. I remember thinking "How does he know what to do? All these lights, how does he know which ones to use and where to point them?" I learned the most about lighting in those early years while leaning over the handrails.

The Forest Set of Camelot, Circa 1967
(Photo Credit: The Film Experience (fair use)

I have always felt that lighting was one of the most creative elements of the collectively creative film making process. The writer, of course, is the one who puts pen to paper and creates the framework in which everyone is bound. Actors are bound to the script and told what to say by the writer; they are told where to stand by the director, and where to look by the cameraman. Directors are bound to the script while staging a scene; they must work with what the writer gives them. Costume designers, make-up artists, set designers, although incredibly creative, are all bound to the script.

Lighting, on the other hand, starts with blackness: A blank canvas. The only things the script tells us is if it is a day or night scene and if it is interior or exterior. We take what the writer, the director, the actors and the set designers give us, and we create a "look." Every scene is lit differently. Every shot is a new challenge. That is what I love about lighting!

The Early TV Shows

During my apprenticeship I worked on many of the Warner Brothers TV shows of the day. I quickly learned the difference between working on a high budget movie like *Camelot* and a TV show like *The Streets of San Francisco*. It takes three to five months to film a 90-minute movie. They film a one-hour TV show in six to eight days or less. Not a lot of time to let the creative juices flow. I once had a tee shirt that read: *THEATER – IS ART, MOVIES – ARE ENTERTAINMENT, TV - IS FURNITURE!*

The TV show *Bonanza*, however, was a prime gig. Their crew

had been together for many years and was a tight-knit family. Wilber Kinnett was the gaffer and had done the show from day one. Maybe I should clarify what the word gaffer means. It is an old English slang term referring to a foreman, a boss or the old man. In modern times gaffer refers to the Chief Lighting Technician on a movie set.

Wilber was a well-known and respected TV gaffer. He was a soft-spoken gentleman who respected his crew. His crew loved him and had been with him for years. The production company was top notch. I lucked out and was able to work on *Bonanza* quite often, not as a regular but as a favorite extra hire. *Bonanza* was the first TV series to go full color on NBC.

**Lead Cast of Bonanza
Circa 1962**

(top to bottom) Lorne Greene, Dan Blocker, Michael Landon and Pernell Roberts

(Photo Credit: Public Domain)

After a fire on their set at Paramount Studios, the producers decided to move the entire production to Warner Brothers. They had a big set that was the outside of the Ponderosa Ranch on one stage and a couple of other stages with interior sets, so most of the show was filmed on stage. Once or twice a year they would go on location up to the Sonora, California, area and shoot some stock footage and a couple of special shows. Michael Landon would later go back to Sonora many times while shooting *Little House on the Prairie*.

The cast were all great guys. Dan Blocker was a big "gentle giant," a wonderful person with a good sense of humor and a great laugh. Lorne Green could be a little pompous but still a nice person. Pernell

5

Roberts was nice but kept to himself. Michael Landon was a kind, caring person and quite the jokester. All of the actors knew the names of all the regular crew members and their families. Every year the Company would have a big Christmas party for the cast and crew and their families. The company would always gift the crew something big; color TV's, bicycles, or a huge Christmas bonus.

It was always pretty low key on the set. One day Michael Landon caught one of the regular electricians sleeping up in the catwalks. He went to the prop guy and got a gun loaded with blanks. He walked over to just under where the guy was sleeping and started calling his name. He shouted, "Manny, wake up!" When Manny finally woke up and looked down where Michael stood, Michael said, "You've fallen asleep for the last time, Manny." He then pointed the gun and fired off a couple of blanks. Manny almost peed himself and had to be relieved so he could go to the men's room. Michael did that kind of thing all the time. It was a terrific show to work on as long as you did not go to sleep on the job.

The script Michael Landon wrote for Dan Blocker, *Forever*, was filmed in 1972 shortly after Dan's death, and Michael both played the part he had written for Dan and directed the episode. Michael cared so much about this episode that he had a screening at Warner Brothers for the crew and cast to view before the show aired.

In 1972, I was hired as the best boy on the first season of *The Streets of San Francisco*. Maybe now is a good time to explain what a best boy is. You may have seen it in the credits as they whirl by at the end of a film. You do watch the credits, don't you? Well, the best boy (Assistant Chief Lighting Technician) is the number two person on the lighting crew right under the lighting gaffer (Chief Lighting Technician.) The gaffer is in charge of the lighting, the best boy is in charge of the lighting equipment and the lighting crew. The best boy makes sure the gaffer has everything he needs to light the set and assigns the tasks to be done. The name best boy comes from the old days at the major studios. Each day the studios would hire hundreds of men for all different types of jobs. The men would all congregate at the studio gate. The gaffers for each show would come out to pick a crew of 75 men or so to work that day. Rather than stand there himself and pick 75 guys from the hundreds gathered there, the gaffer would pick one guy out of the crowd, usually someone he knew or someone who had worked for him before, and designate him as the "best of the boys." The best boy would then pick the crew.

Anyway, back to *The Streets of San Francisco*. It was my first best boy job, but the only reason I got it was because none of the ol' timers wanted it. The schedule was pretty grueling. We would film 10 days (half of two episodes) in San Francisco and then 10 days (the other half of the same two episodes) in and around Los Angeles and at the studio. In later years, they stopped the split schedule and filmed it all in San Francisco.

Lead Cast Streets of San Francisco
Circa 1967
Karl Malden, Michael Douglas
(Photo Credit: Public Domain)

A lot of times, if the assistant director was short of extras, he/she would ask the crew if they wanted to work as extras. Sometimes it was not a bad gig. You get your regular pay plus they pay you the extra's daily minimum. But it is not always a good deal because you had to work to light the set then you had to work in the shot. Then you had to work to light the set for the next shot. You got no time to rest. I've worked as an extra in the background on many shows, but my film debut was on *The Streets of San Francisco* as a long-haired hippie sitting in a biker bar. At least it was a sit down job.

The Streets of San Francisco was a Quinn Martin production. Quinn Martin was one of the most prolific American television producers for decades. He had at least one television series running in prime time every year for 21 straight years, an industry record, and he filmed most of them at Warner Brothers. I worked off and on for another Quinn Martin production at Warners, *The FBI.* That was another really tight crew who had worked together for a long time. The gaffer was Bob Farmer who would later become the head of the Set Lighting Department at Warner Brothers.

Lead Cast The FBI, Circa 1965
(L to R): William Reynolds, Efrem Zimbalist Jr., Phillip Abbot
(Photo Credit: Public Domain)

Efrem Zimbalist Jr. was really cool. He was suave, debonair, and a real gentleman. He knew all the crew (they had been working together for years.) He had a great sense of humor and loved a good gag. The original episodes were filmed in black and white because there were very few color TVs. In the early 70s they switched to color.

The evolution of color film in the movie industry, and later the TV industry, was an enormous change for lighting. We had to light differently for color than for black and white. We could no longer light for various shades of white to gray to black with high contrast like we did with black and white film. We now had to light a wider mid-range of color, the contrast now being accomplished through different light intensities. We also then needed to have two completely different types of lights; the warm colored lights (3200° Kelvin) that we had always used for black and white filming and cool blue lights (5500° Kelvin) for daytime outdoor shooting.

Maybe I should explain Kelvin temperature. Kelvin temperature is a rating of light color in varying degrees from red (or infra-red) being the lowest temperature, or warmest Kelvin rating, to blue (or ultra-violet) being the highest temperature, or coolest, Kelvin rating. So, warm light is low temperature and cool light is high temperature. Go figure! Color movie film and our lights were both rated warm at 3200° Kelvin. Daylight is on the cool blue side of the light spectrum at approx. 5500° Kelvin. Because the camera always uses the same warm rated 3200° Kelvin color film indoors and outdoors, for daylight filming, the cameraman has to put an orange colored filter on the lens to correct the film to the blue daylight. In addition, we need to use blue (5500° Kelvin) lights to match the daylight Kelvin temperature.

The problem was that as the TV shows started to go to color, the studios did not have enough of the blue outdoor day lights for both the movies and the TV productions. What Warner Brothers had instead were blue glass filters, called Macbeth's, for the old studio indoor warm lights. So, when you would go from the studio to location, you had to put these big blue glass filters on all the indoor studio lights to correct them to daylight. Later the studio started investing in newer equipment but it was really too late. The studio system was dying as the independent producers were taking over the industry. More on that later.

Another TV show I worked on at the time was *The Partridge Family*. They filmed it at the Columbia ranch lot in Burbank. This was another show that had been running for a few years and the cast and crew were really tight.

David Cassidy

David Cassidy was the teen idol of the day so there was always a large group of screaming girls at the studio gate waiting for a glimpse of him, and usually all they got to see were crew members driving into the crew parking lot. Most times David's driver would take him through the back gate. Sometimes though he would drive through the main gate and give the girls a peek. You could hear the screaming girls a mile away.

Shirley Jones was a sweet, charming, delightful person. She would come on the stage and stop and talk to almost everybody on the crew. I was just part time on the show, but she would recognize me and say "Hi" to me too. At the wrap party on stage, she treated us to an impromptu, a cappella version of *Out of My Dreams* from *Oklahoma*. What a once in a lifetime experience!

Shirley Jones

Danny Bonaduce

Danny Bonaduce was a precocious little boy. I am afraid we might have contributed to his juvenile delin-quency, though. We used to egg him on to do stuff that we knew he would get in trouble for, and he did. Poor Danny, sorry bro!

On one of the episodes I worked on we filmed on board a cruise ship to the Mexican Riviera. We did not get the full cruise, you understand, we only got half the cruise because it was a 10-day cruise and we only had 5 days of shooting to do. We joined the ship half way in Ensenada, Mexico, and filmed on the way back to San Pedro,

California. Without any prodding from us, not surprisingly, Danny got himself confined to quarters by the ship's captain, something about harassing the passengers.

The production company did not want to tell the Mexican government that we were working in Mexican waters or while tied up in Mexican ports to avoid paying any kind of port fee or tax. That worked fine for them, but we had to lie to the Border Patrol and tell them we were in Mexico for pleasure not business. It also meant that we could not bring any of our tools. We had to borrow the tools we needed from some of the ship mechanics. I had to hook our cable into the ship's power panel every morning. "Kid, go hook us up" (the new guy on a show was always called "Kid"). The pliers I borrowed from one of the shipmates in the engine room were not insulated, and I had no gloves. I was standing on a damp metal deck outside the engine room, so I knew I was going to "get bit," but I had to do it anyway. I started hooking up our cables but there was a load on the line so as soon as I completed the circuit the 120-volt current surged through my body and threw me backwards about 10 feet. The only thing that kept me from being thrown overboard was the fact that I had my back facing down the walkway and not toward the deck rail. Boy that hurt!!! One of the other shipmates had a better pair of pliers and some gloves so I eventually was able to hook us up.

Another movie I worked on as part of my early career was *The Omega Man* starring Charlton Heston, Anthony Zerbe and Rosalind Cash. The gaffer was Lee Wilson, one of my favorite gaffers. I had the pleasure of working with him part-time on several shows in those early years; he was one of Warner Brothers' top gaffers. I learned so much from Lee Wilson. Not only about lighting but about how you treat a crew. He was such a gentleman. He treated everyone with respect. He was one of the good guys in a cut-throat business. His best boy was a wonderful man named Buddy Boes. He, too, was a real gentleman. They were a great team. I learned a lot about being a good best boy from watching Buddy Boes.

Many times, when I was working at Warner Brothers, I would go to lunch at a little restaurant close to the studio called Papoo's Hot Dog Show. It was across from the famous Toluca Lake Bob's Big Boy restaurant. One day, I got my Hot Dog Show Chili Dog Deluxe and went to sit in the small dining room in the back.

As I got close to the door, I heard people laughing. When I walked in, I saw that Jonathan Winters was front and center going through an entire comedy routine for 15 people. He continued for another 30 minutes then took a bow, shook everybody's hand and left (he lived close by) It was incredible. He had a genius comedic mind for improvisation. He was a mentor for comedians like Robin Williams.

I FINALLY MAKE IT TO THE BIGS

DELIVERANCE (1971)

Starring:	Jon Voight, Burt Reynolds, Ned Beatty and Ronny Cox
Director:	John Boorman
Cinematographer:	Vilmos Zsigmond
Lighting Gaffer:	Jim Blair

I was 26 years old and had been in the business about five years. I was working at Warner Brothers when this new movie titled *Deliverance* came up to be filmed on location. You have to understand the big studio machine in those days. The studios and the studio unions back then had a seniority preference list of all their "ol' timers" who had worked there for many years. They had their pick of all the shows and we "kids" were relegated to the "rigging crew" or any TV show the preference men did not want.

Distant location work was the cream of the crop because we worked six days a week, Saturday at time and a half, and we got paid 8 hours for Sunday. Do not get me wrong, I am a 100% union man, but the preference list was discriminatory, and we "kids," and the federal government, were instrumental in getting it abolished. So, when this new location came up, the Studio was told that it was going to be filmed on one of the wildest rivers in America and the producers insisted that the studio not send any of their ol' timers. This gave us "kids" a foot in the door.

We filmed *Deliverance* in northeast Georgia mostly on the Chattooga River from May through July of 1971. The Chattooga River at that time was one of the country's wildest rivers with rapids called "Widow Shoals" and "Sokem Dog." We stayed in Clayton, Georgia, at the Heart of Rabun Motel. I did not like my room very much. It was a small room in an inside hallway with no windows, plus I had to room with another guy on the crew. A couple of weeks into the show, several crew members were complaining on the set about missing T-shirts. One of the guy's wives said she saw one of the maids stuffing T-shirts into her laundry bag. When a couple of us complained to the manager about the maids stealing our T-shirts, the manager said we were lying and threw us out of the motel.

We ended up staying at The Dillard House, an antebellum hotel in town owned by Lucille Dillard, the woman who also catered our lunches on the set. Lucille was a sweetheart and a great "Southern" cook, but she served us chicken, in some form or another, every single day for lunch. We never complained because it was always good, but it was always chicken. One day Lucille told us she had a special Hungarian recipe she was cooking for dinner that night in honor of Vilmos Zsigmond. As we sat in her restaurant dining room anticipating Hungarian Goulash or some other exotic Hungarian epicurean delight, Lucille presented us with her "Hungarian Chicken"!!!

Most of the rest of the people of Clayton did not like us much at first. The local church group got a copy of the book and read about this homosexual rape scene with a mountain man, so we were all branded as "rich Hollywood queers." Sometimes when our crew bus would come into town after a hard day's work on the river, we could see the local restaurants turn their signs from open to closed as we passed. One restaurant had a printed "No Dogs Allowed" sign in the window that they had penciled in to read "No Dogs, No ("N"-word), and No Movie People Allowed." There was a huge billboard on the highway into town that said "JOIN THE KKK, CALL BILLY BOB AT ----." Like I said this was 1971.

As a white boy from Burbank, California, this was the first time I had encountered prejudice against me. I was standing in line at a local grocery store check-out when the little boy in front of me turned to his mother and said, "Look, mommy, there's one of them damn Yankees from Hollywood." As time went on, Lucille convinced the rest of the local merchants that we had a lot of money to spend and the only place we could spend it was in Clayton. They all suddenly changed their tune… Money talks!

One of our first locations was the house where the little boy plays the banjo. His name was Billy Joe Redden, and he was 15 years old. We were told he was inbred, and he lived with his extended family in the hills nearby. He was a nice little kid, full of wonder about all the things he was seeing for the first time. At the lunch table, we showed him how to peel an orange and how to eat a banana. He loved it. He had never seen anything like that. If they could not grow it or shoot it, they did not eat it.

Ronny Cox could play the guitar, but Billy Joe could not play the banjo. In the scene it appears Billy Joe is actually playing the banjo. He is not. In the close-ups there was another little 15-year-old boy (who never even got screen credit) crouched down behind the swing Billy Joe is sitting on. The costume people had cut the back of Billy Joe's shirt so that the boy behind the swing could put his left arm through the sleeve. On camera Billy Joe just pretended to strum the banjo with his right hand while the boy behind the swing actually plays the frets. It looks pretty convincing. Movie magic!

Speaking of movie magic, Vilmos Zsigmond the cinematographer on the film, was a genius. He was known for his use of light and color to give life to a film. One of his earlier films was *McCabe and Mrs. Miller*. Every shot in that film is a masterpiece of art. He had an incredible eye for light.

On a historical side note, Vilmos and his best friend Laszlo Kovacs (I will be talking a lot more about Laszlo later) were film students in Budapest, Hungary, when the Russian army invaded in 1956. They "borrowed" an Arraflex camera and some film from the university and, at great personal risk, filmed what ended up being the only footage that was ever seen of the Russian tanks rolling through the city of Budapest. How they developed the film and smuggled it out of the country would make a good movie in itself.

In the opening sequence in *Deliverance*, the men pull in to an old rundown gas station. That set was part of someone's house, not a gas station. The art director brought in the old gas pumps and some old junk cars and all the gas station set dressing. After we were through filming, they came back and removed all their set dressing. They took all the junk cars to the scrap yard and had them crushed. It turned out one of the junk cars was the family car of the people that lived in the house. They got a new car.

One of the local people they hired to act in this scene had a nervous whistle. The other actors would be talking and he would be standing there whistling with every exhale. It was a very short scene so the director just lived with it. During the scene one of the men takes a look around the place. He looks in a window and sees an old woman with a young girl who is disabled in her lap. They actually lived there. This scene was added to the script on the spot.

The rape scene was a very difficult scene to shoot in several aspects. It was a complicated scene to set up because John Boorman had laid it out to be filmed mostly in one shot. This, of course, presents a challenge to us "light guys" to keep all of our lights out of the picture as the camera moves around the set. It took most of the morning to set up the scene. The mood on the set that day was uncharacteristically somber. Violent scenes like this are sometimes very difficult to have to watch for someone who has to be on the set. You sometimes feel like you are a witness to a violent act, and you cannot stop it. You can only stand there and watch. You sometimes feel like a victim. I have had this same feeling other times on other shows during my career. It can be very disturbing.

Other than our four principal actors, Bill McKinney was the only other professional actor in the show. His performance as the mountain man in this very difficult scene was incredible. He played the character perfectly, and I think he gave one of the best dying performances on film. With an arrow through him, he staggers around then comes to rest on some branches with his eyes open. He had to hold his breath and not move a muscle for several minutes during that take. I know I could not do it.

The other mountain man in the scene was named "Cowboy" Coward. Cowboy was quite the character. Unlike the rest of the non-professional people they used in the show, he was not a local. Burt met him in a Wild West stunt show at a theme park in North Carolina where Burt used to work and suggested him for this part because he had a bridge on his front teeth, and he was willing to be filmed with it out, which most professional actors would never do. Cowboy was just a good ol' boy who drank beer pretty much all day and all night. He drank cans of Pabst Blue Ribbon Beer, "Ol' Blue" he called it. When we were setting up the scene where Jon Voight lowers Cowboys' lifeless body over the edge of the cliff and down to the water, we were using a life-size ragdoll dummy to stand-in for Cowboy. At first, they thought they could shoot the scene using the dummy but it just did not look real enough. So, John Boorman asked Cowboy if he thought he could do the stunt himself and Cowboy said, "Well if that dummy can do it, I sure as hell can."

The rapids scene where Burt Reynolds' character gets his leg broken (they went to the local butcher shop and bought a lamb leg bone, and that is what you see sticking out of his leg), was filmed in Tallulah Gorge. The gorge is a mile long and 1000 feet deep. We, of course, had to get all of our equipment and us down those 1000 feet. They ran a cable from the east rim down to the west bank of the river to shuttle our lights, cameras, sound equipment and Lucille's chicken down to the set. The crew had to go down (and back up) a very steep slope on the west rim using a rope hand over hand. It took a couple of weeks to shoot all the scenes there so we did this every day for about two weeks.

There was a dam a couple of miles upstream from the gorge that controls the flow of the river. The normal river flow was not strong enough to make the rapids look dangerous enough. John Boorman wanted more water. The location manager had arranged with the people at the dam to be able to open some gates on the dam to allow more water downstream. John asked how many gates there were on the dam. The dam supervisor told him there were 12 gates. John said "OK then let's open one gate." It took several minutes for the water to reach where we were so there we stood, lights, cameras, director, actors in the water waiting to shoot the scene where they crash down the rapids. Suddenly, we heard the sound of roaring water echoing down the gorge. We were looking upstream with nervous anticipation, when from around a bend in the river upstream, we saw our worst nightmare, a ten-foot-high wall of water coming our way. We all started grabbing our lights and cameras out of the water and scrambled for high ground. We lost one of the wooden canoes and some other props, but luckily no one was hurt. During the course of the show, we destroyed five wooden canoes. When we actually filmed the scene, they only opened one-quarter of a gate. I have included photos that show the difference in the flow of water through the gorge. These photos depict what happened when the water came up.

Ronnie Cox's character's body was found downstream in an area of the river they called "Sokem Dog." When they find him, his one arm is dislocated and twisted around his head. This was no special effect. Ronnie could actually dislocate his shoulder and twist it around his head!

It really looked weird.

Needless to say, we did a lot of filming on or in the water, so we needed to use DC power because DC current, unlike AC current, does not go to ground so it is safe to use in water. The industry at the time was still using DC current exclusively so, we had a DC generator plus a couple of 120v battery packs (ten, 12volt batteries hooked up in series to equal 120volts). We used some new DC lights called Xenons. Their bulb contained Xenon gas which, when ignited, creates the high intensity light needed to shoot outdoors. The lights were basically a cylindrical shape and came with the warning that water splashed on the front of the hot lamp could cause the Xenon bulb to explode like a rocket launcher and spew deadly Xenon gas everywhere. Other than that, there was no problem. What could possibly go wrong? We were very careful!

We could not shoot the underwater scenes in the river because the water was not clear enough, so we used the local community pool. The pool water, however, was not clear enough either, but they could correct that by draining the pool and refilling it with fresh water. Our special effects guys drained the pool and refilled it. The trouble was they did not contact the local plumber who was in charge of draining and refilling the community pool. The other snag was the fact that the plumber was also the Mayor, so we had to pay him to drain and refill the pool one more time.

James Dickey, the man who wrote the book and the screenplay talked them into letting him play the Sheriff in the movie. He was better known as a poet and I'm sure he was a better poet than actor. He was, to say the least, a very strange man. John Boorman ended up barring him from the set because he was confusing the actors, trying to direct them.

Dickey told everyone that everything that happened in the book actually happened to him. But, John Boorman said that when he went canoeing down the river for the original location scouting with Jim Dickey, he capsized the canoe. It was obvious then that he had never been in a canoe in his life and that probably none of what happened in the book actually happened to him.

Dickey also made the production company hire his young son, Christopher Dickey, as a stand-in. I do not think Christopher had a very good time on his paid summer vacation with his father. He later became a well-known and well-respected journalist. He wrote a book called *Summer of Deliverance* in which he writes about his tumultuous relationship with his "alcoholic, womanizing father." He also wrote that he felt the crew on the movie was disgruntled and angry about being there. I think he was projecting his unhappiness on us. This was one of the best crews I ever worked with. It was a very difficult show to film but we all had a great time.

On another side note, John Boorman had brought his family over from England along with a young man named Tony Adams. Tony was employed as a tutor/nanny for John's children. I got to know Tony very well. He was an Irish kid just looking to make it in Hollywood. After the show we had Tony over to our house one night for dinner. He told us John introduced him to his friends Julie Andrews and Blake Edwards. Tony ended up staying with them at their Malibu beach home, eventually becoming the producer of all of Blake Edwards's subsequent films. He made it in Hollywood and never looked back. I would work with Tony some 15 years later on a Blake Edwards show, *Sunset,* but Tony did not seem to know me or remember our kindness at a time when he needed a free meal. Oh well, that's show biz!

Deliverance - The Cast

Burt Reynolds

Ned Beatty

Jon Voight

Ronny Cox

Billy Joe Redden

Bill McKinney

21

Deliverance - The Cast & Crew

The Crew
(Photo Credit: Jim Coe)

The Crew at the Gorge

Cowboy and James Dickey

Jim Blair, Gaffer, Aaron Pazanti, Best Boy, Paul Caven

Jim Blair, Vilmos Zsigmond & Aaron Pazanti at the Gorge

Paul Caven "The Kid"

Deliverance - The Cast & Crew In Action

Filming the Campsite Scene

Burt Reynolds & Jon Voight

23

Burt Reynolds & Ned Beatty First Rapids

Jon Voight & Ronny Cox First Rapids

Ralph Garret Stuntman

What follows are three photos with circles added to show what happened when the water came up in the Gorge. The circles show a couple of members of the prop crew that were in the stream waiting to release a broken canoe with a dummy, dressed as Burt, for the shot where Burt crashes and gets hurt. Another couple of prop guys are on the other side with another canoe. During the sequence you can see the two guys with the broken canoe at one point just drop the canoe and scramble to the side. In the third photo you see the prop crew has scrambled to high ground while the rest of us struggle to get our equipment and ourselves up a ladder to high ground. (These photos were taken by a member of the crew with my camera.)

The Gorge Empty
Prop Guys with Canoes

The Gorge Medium
Swimming to high ground

25

The Gorge Full
The rest of us going up a ladder to high ground

WHAT'S UP DOC (1971)

Starring:	Barbra Streisand, Ryan O'Neal, Madeline Kahn, Kenneth Mars, Austin Pendleton, John Hillerman
Director:	Peter Bogdanovich
Writer:	Buck Henry
Cinematographer:	Laszlo Kovacs
Lighting Gaffer:	Aggie Aguilar

What's Up Doc was my first film with Laszlo Kovacs and his legendary Gaffer, Richmond "Aggie" Aguilar. They were a team. They had worked together for many years on lots of low budget movies including one low budget biker movie of particular note: *Easy Rider.*

What's Up Doc had an extraordinary cast. Barbra and Ryan had an amazing chemistry and an exceptional sense of comedic timing. This was the film debut of Madeline Kahn, and she was nominated for a Golden Globe for best newcomer. Madeline was a natural, and she went on to have a wonderful career, including working with Peter a couple of more times. Kenneth Mars, Austin Pendleton, Sorrell Booke, and Michael Murphy filled in the rest of this uncommon cast of characters. The long-haired, redheaded bicycle delivery boy in the show is Ryan's brother Kevin O'Neal, and the woman Barbra sits next to on the plane in the last scene is Ryan and Kevin's mother, Patricia O'Neal.

We filmed from July to October of 1971 in San Francisco and on stage at Warner Brothers studio. We filmed the first four weeks in San Francisco filming the airport scenes and all the exterior scenes except for the chase scene. In other words, we had to shoot all the airport scenes, including the last scene which happens after the chase scene in the script. The last scene involves all the major characters in the chase scene and the dialog refers to things that happen in the chase scene, all before we filmed the chase scene. At that time, not much of the chase scene had even been written. When we did shoot the chase scene a lot of what happened was spontaneous, so it was very difficult for the actors to try to relate to circumstances that had not happened yet.

27

We filmed for another four weeks on stage at Warner Brothers. We had two or three stages with the hotel hallway and room sets, the party set, and the banquet set. Peter did some incredible stuff in this picture. His style was to play as much of the scene as possible in one shot. He preferred to have a camera move in to a close up, not zoom in to a close up. He followed the flow of the scene with the camera. Not many directors have the command of the camera that Peter has. He was a student of Hollywood's all-time classic directors like Orson Wells, Howard Hawks, and Alfred Hitchcock.

Not many directors today know how to use the camera, so they just go through the basics: wide shot, medium shot, two close-ups, back to the wide shot, cue the car crash and explosion. Physical comedy is very difficult to shoot. Not only do the actors need to sell it, but the camera needs to be in position to see it. During the banquet scene, Peter played a large part of the scene with the actors under a table. That is what I mean about following the flow of the scene with the camera. Peter employed every slapstick gag from the silent days as well as the sophisticated comedies of the 1930s and 1940s. It is said that this film was loosely based on the wonderful Cary Grant and Katharine Hepburn movie *Bringing Up Baby*. Ryan definitely channels Cary Grant in this film.

In one scene Barbra's character is out on the ledge of the hotel at night. She slips and is hanging on to the ledge for dear life. Donna Garrett was Barbra's stunt double. Donna was a pioneer for women stunt performers. It used to be that men would be used as stunt doubles for actresses. Donna broke the glass ceiling for stuntwomen in the Stuntmen's Association. She was the best. I worked with her husband Ralph Garrett on *Deliverance*. Ralph was Jon Voight's stunt double. He did the rock-climbing stunts, plus it is Ralph's hand that comes up out of the water in the last shot of the movie. The Garretts used to throw the best New Year's Eve parties.

Anyway, to get back to my story, Donna and the stunt crew worked all day setting up the stunt. They ran safety cables, they hooked up her harness; all was set up to make sure Donna would be perfectly safe. When it came time to shoot it that evening, Donna ran through a final rehearsal for camera. As she was hanging from the ledge, Laszlo decided he needed one more light on her. Being the rookie on the crew, I was selected. "Here kid take this light up there and shine it on Donna." So, I ran up to the 10th floor of the hotel, and hung out a window that was out of the shot, in order to better light Donna. They spent all day hooking Donna up to make sure she was safe, but when we filmed it, I was standing on a window sill 10 stories up holding on to the three-foot-wide window frame with one hand and holding the light out as far as I could with the other hand. There's no business-like show business!

We went back to San Francisco for the last four weeks of shooting to film the chase scene. We filmed all over the city. The famous glass panel scene was filmed on Balboa St. and 22nd Ave. It took all day to set it up and 10 seconds to shoot it. It was a fabulous stunt. The Chinatown scene was really something. They made this huge dragon to be part of this make-believe Chinese New Year's parade. There, of course, was no parade but all the people you see on the sidewalk watching the "parade" were actually there watching us shoot. Free extras! The other weird thing is that Peter had the Chinese High School Band that is in the parade play *La Cucaracha*. Go figure!

A lot of the chase stunts were set up on the spot. Someone would suggest an idea for a stunt and we would shoot it. The scene where Barbra walks across the street to the hotel and causes a car crash is a prime example. The script did not call for a car crash but Peter thought it would be a great gag. The problem was they did not have any stunt cars available that day, so Peter sent his personal assistant, Frank Marshall, to a local car rental place to rent two cars. He told him to make sure to buy the collision insurance. I would like to have been a fly on the wall when they returned those two cars with major damage.

Another example of "seat-of-your-pants" film making was when they decided to run all the chase cars down the concrete steps in Alta Plaza Park. If you watch closely you can see the major damage this causes. You can see big chunks of concrete flying. The damage is still evident today. If you have ever walked down those steps and wondered why they were so chipped, you can thank the stunt coordinator who said, "Yeah, we can do that." Because of the damage to the Alta Plaza Park steps, the City of San Francisco, as well as many other cities, now require movie productions to provide a very detailed scene-by-scene breakdown of everything they plan to do. Hurray for Hollywood!

I would like to share with you a few other side notes related to the crew on this production. The painter on the roof top scene is Len

Lookabaugh, the "dolly grip" on the show. Frank Marshall was the assistant to Peter Bogdanovich and the guy who rented the two cars. He would work with Peter on a few more shows but eventually he connected with Steven Spielberg and became his producer. He produced the *Indiana Jones* series of movies as well as the fatal *Twilight Zone* movie. Another production assistant on the show was Neil Canton. Neil was a nice, quiet, soft spoken kid. I think this was his first picture. He went on to produce many films including all of the *Back to the Future* series. I would work with both Frank and Neil on three more Peter Bogdanovich shows. I knew them when...

I worked on a total of five pictures with Peter Bogdanovich. He is one of my all-time favorite directors. This was my first of 25 pictures with the genius of light, the maestro, Laszlo Kovacs. I would do over 30 movies and countless commercials with his renowned lighting gaffer Aggie Aguilar. Aggie took a liking to me and we worked together for the next 25 years until his retirement.

What's Up Doc? – Cinematographer and Gaffer

Laszlo Kovacs   Aggie Aguilar

What's Up Doc? – The Cast

Ryan O'Neal

Barbra Streisand

What's Up Doc? – The Crew in Action

Camera Car

Plate Glass Stunt

Bicycle Cart Stunt

KING OF MARVIN GARDENS (1971-1972)

Starring: Jack Nicholson, Bruce Dern, Ellen Burstyn, Julia Anne Robinson, Scatman Crothers

Director: Bob Rafelson

Cinematographer: Laszlo Kovacs

Lighting Gaffer: Jim Blair

The working title for this movie while we were shooting was *The Philosopher King.* I think I prefer the title they settled on after shooting. We filmed in Atlantic City, New Jersey, and Philadelphia from December 1971 through February 1972.

Aggie could not do this film so the gaffer was Jim Blair. We filmed most of the movie in and around Atlantic City, New Jersey. We stayed at the Howard-Johnson's located one block off the boardwalk with a great view of the Atlantic Ocean. Out of our hotel room window, my wife, Denise, noticed a little hamburger joint down the street. She marveled about how many cars, limos and cabs stopped there and within a couple of minutes left. This went on all day long. We thought they must make a great burger. Later we found out it was a bookie joint.

Atlantic City was in the process of dying a slow and painful death in the winter of 1971. In its glory days, Atlantic City was the place to be on the Jersey shore. It had beautiful, massive hotel palaces on a boardwalk that was miles long. There was also the Steel Pier amusement park, and the Miss America Pageant. It was also the home of the board game Monopoly. We went around and found all the streets, from Boardwalk to Park Place. The streets on the game board are all in Atlantic City, except for Marvin Gardens. Marven Gardens (it is misspelled on the board game) is in the town of Margate City two miles south of Atlantic City.

By 1971, the area was crime ridden and economically depressed. That, of course, worked perfectly as the backdrop for this dark, gritty drama of sibling dysfunction. It is said that *King of Marvin Gardens* is considered a Jack Nicholson cult classic. Jack, as always, delivers a marvelous performance, but I think Bruce Dern and Ellen Burstyn also deserve great credit. This was Julia Anne Robinson's only major film role. She died tragically at the age of twenty-four in an apartment fire two years after this film's release.

We filmed all the hotel scenes at the Marlborough-Blenheim Hotel on the corner of Boardwalk and Park Place. The Blenheim was one of the dinosaurs left over from the glory days. It was a marvelous old boardwalk hotel, the manifestation of glamour and opulence. It was sad to see such a grand old hotel fall into such disrepair. Within a few years, legalized gambling came to Atlantic City, and by 1979, the Marlborough-Blenheim Hotel was demolished and the Bally's Park Place Casino rose from the ashes. The rest is history. I just wonder how long it will take for these new gambling palaces to become passé.

Jack Nicholson is one of my favorite actors. He, more than most current actors, was just one of the guys. Crew members rate actors by how they relate to the crew. Experienced actors understand that this is a collectively creative medium. We are all involved and everyone wants it to be the best film on their resume. Actors who think it is all about them usually end up shunned by the crew. This can lead to unflattering close-ups.

It was wintertime and this was the first time this little California boy ever saw snow on the beach…how weird. There was nothing to do in Atlantic City, so the company set up a couple of ping-pong tables in one of Howard Johnson's meeting rooms so we could play and let off some steam after work. Jack, as you may imagine, is very competitive. He spent a lot of time there. He would take on all comers. He is the best ping-pong player I have ever seen and he kicked everybody's butt.

The hotel food was so bad that the company hired a caterer to feed us breakfast and dinner. The caterer set up in the banquet kitchen and served us in the bar. I am not sure if Jack was on a diet, but I never saw him get his own plate. Most nights, he would come in the bar, go to each of our tables and talk for a few minutes and eat part of our meals. The majority of the conversation was about the L.A. Lakers. One night he came in with the news that the Lakers had just broken the NBA record with a 33-game winning streak. We all celebrated with champagne on Jack.

Bruce Dern was cool too. He was a jogger. He would go out early every morning and jog up and down the boardwalk. He was kind of a health food nut. Speaking of nuts, he was the first person I ever saw who put salted peanuts in his Coke, not exactly health food. During the Miss America scene, Ellen and Julia Anne fell off the back of the golf cart Bruce was driving when he took off too fast. Julia Anne hit her head and spent a few days in the hospital as a result.

Ellen Burstyn was incredible. What she did with this pathetic but sympathetic character was genius. She really brought the character to life. She, of course, went on later to win Academy Awards, Tony Awards, and Golden Globe Awards. She is an astonishing actress and a sweet person.

Scatman Crothers wrote that this role was his favorite role of his career. Jack Nicholson and Scatman Crothers appeared together later in *The Fortune* (1975), *One Flew Over The Cuckoo's Nest* (1975), and *The Shining* (1980).

The King of Marvin Gardens: Director and Assistant Director

Bob Rafelson & Michael Haley

Laszlo Kovacs

The King of Marvin Gardens – The Cast

Jack Nicholson & Bruce Dern

Jack Nicholson

PAPER MOON (1972)

Starring:	Ryan O'Neal, Tatum O'Neal, Madeline Kahn, John Hillerman, P.J. Johnson
Director:	Peter Bogdanovich
Cinematographer:	Laszlo Kovacs
Lighting Gaffer:	Aggie Aguilar

Paper Moon was nominated for a Golden Globe for Best Picture. Peter, Ryan, Tatum and Madeline were all nominated for Golden Globes. Tatum won the Academy Award, and Madeline was nominated for an Academy Award. For my money, this is Peter Bogdanovich's best picture. He insisted that it be filmed in black and white. Genius! He wanted to depict the stark, depression era, *Grapes of Wrath* like, Midwest of the 1930s.

He wanted a high contrast look so Laszlo used a red filter to accomplish this. That, of course, posed a challenge for us lighting guys because the red filter adds 2 f-stops to the camera, so we need 2 f-stops more light. Peter also wanted to have a deep depth of field. This means that everything in the shot is in focus. In other words, the foreground and the background are both in focus. You can see this in many scenes where we are shooting inside, but outside through the window you see background action that is also in focus. You achieve this by using a high f-stop on the camera, plus we needed to provide 2 f-stops more light to compensate for the red filter. For us "sparkies," this movie was all about light.

Peter also perfected his style of "all-in-one shot" film making. He called it "cutting with the camera." In other words, when you shoot scenes all in one shot, there is no need to edit it or cut it. He did, however, hire one of the best editors in Hollywood, Verna Fields, because when a film is shot that way, there is no extra footage to be able to cut to, so a really good editor is essential.

Peter likes the camera to flow with the action in the scene. When everything is in focus, you can show separation in your characters without having to throw the focus back and forth between the actor in

37

the foreground and the actor in the background or have to cut to close ups. Because of all the extra light we used, the camera can move in for a close up, and everything is in focus. Again, genius!

Peter likes to use a lot of the same people in every movie, not only a lot of the same actors (Ryan O'Neal, Madeline Kahn, John Hillerman, and Randy Quaid) but a lot of the same crew. This was his third picture with Laszlo and his camera crew, lighting crew and grip crew. Peter's soon-to-be-ex-wife, Polly Platt, worked on all of his early films as a production designer as well as the costume designer on this film. Frank Marshall and Neil Canton were also on this show. Peter liked working with people he knew.

The actress playing Imogene was a 15-year-old schoolgirl from Houston, Texas, named P. J. Johnson. She had traveled to Dallas to audition for Peter, but before her audition started, she walked right up to Peter and said, "Ooo-WEE! You good lookin!" Impressed with her guts, he responded by saying, "You just got the part."

We filmed in and around Hays, Kansas, and then St. Joseph, Missouri, from September to December of 1972. We stayed at the Holiday Inn in Hays. After work, a lot of us would hang out in the hotel bar. On the weekends, the bar seemed to attract a lot of the local girls looking to hook up with one of the "movie guys."

That worked fine for a lot of our guys, but not so well for some of the local boys. It all came to a head on Halloween night. The local boys made their stand. Push came to shove and the next thing I knew we were in the middle of a genuine barroom fight. All of a sudden, chairs started flying, mirrors were breaking, and glasses were shattered. You could not have staged a better stunt fight for a movie. One of the local guys grabbed Mark, one of our prop guys, by the arms from behind and just as one of his buddies was about to hit him, Mark ducked and the guy hit his buddy and broke his nose.

Some of the girls were not happy with their now ex-boyfriends. I guess they failed to see the chivalry involved. I saw one of the girls jump on her boyfriend's back and start hitting him over the head with a beer bottle. She rode him piggy-back all the way out to the parking lot, with him trying to shake her off, all the while she was bashing him over the head with the bottle. Luckily for us, there were more of us than them, so the carnage did not last long. The local boys high-tailed it, but most of the girls stayed. Nobody was seriously injured, and later some of the local boys would start hanging out with us too. But we did manage to trash the joint; that cost the production company a couple of bucks! However, they did not ban us from the bar because they were making more money than they ever had before. When Peter found out about the mayhem, he said he was "proud of his boys."

We filmed in a number of little towns and on a lot of back roads. One day while we were setting up one of the car scenes on a deserted back road, Tatum O'Neal kept getting in the way. She liked hanging out with the crew, but this time she was being a pest. One of the guys got a long chain and a padlock. We grabbed Tatum and chained her to a tree. Before you start calling Children's Services on us, you must understand that Tatum was laughing the whole time and even had to hold the chain up (it was not cinched very tight). We let her go in time to shoot her scene. I think she just enjoyed us giving her the attention she rarely got from her father.

Another time, a bunch of us took Tatum bowling at the local bowling alley. We could not convince Tatum that she had to wait until the little bar comes up from in front of the pins before you throw your ball down the alley. The owner of the alley did not find it amusing that she kept hitting the little bar with the ball. We had to leave.

The carnival scene was particularly difficult for us to light. It was the perfect storm. We filmed it at night; we always use more lights to shoot at night. Laszlo was using two red filters on the camera for extra high contrast, adding four *f*-stops; more light. Peter wanted everything in focus; even more light. Plus, we filmed the majority of the scene in one shot, so we needed to be sure we kept all our lights out of the shot. It took us a day and a half to light the scene and two nights to shoot it. Another problem with an all-in-one filmed scene is that the actors have to play the whole scene without flubbing a line or missing a mark. I do not know how many dozens of takes we did on that first night, but Tatum ended up getting sick from eating too much cotton candy and had to go home. We came back the next night and filmed it a couple dozen more times. It is a fabulous shot, well worth the hard work.

In the old days, when a company went on a distant location, they would take a full crew. By the 1970s and 1980s most studio production companies were still taking a full Hollywood crew on location; however, the independent producers suddenly realized that being a union show meant that they did not have to take a full crew on location, they could hire local people anywhere they worked as long as they were in the union. Our international union, the International Alliance of Theatrical Stage Employee covers every facet of the entertainment industry in the country. So, they started just taking key people plus a couple of crew people and all the rest of the crew would be hired from the local union wherever they were filming.

Hiring locals worked alright if they were going to be filming in a big city that had theaters and a stagehand local union. Stagehands at least have knowledge of the basics of lighting; they just use different equipment than we do so, we just had to teach them how to use our lights. On *Paper Moon* our home base was the small town of Hays, Kansas, where there were no stagehand locals. All they had was a projectionist local union. Projectionists have no knowledge of lighting concepts or our equipment. The only equipment they have that is vaguely similar to ours is their projectors. Projectors used the same technology as our arc lights to create high intensity light; two sticks of carbon. They, of course, had never operated one of our arc lights or any of our lights, so, we had to teach them the basics.

This approach resulted in our members going on location with a minimum crew and teaching the local union how to do our job. That was alright; at least we are all in the same union. That worked great for all the stagehand locals around the country. They started getting more and more work on films. The bigger cities started their own film workers unions. Cities like New York, Chicago, Atlanta and San Francisco no longer allow production companies to bring any crew from Hollywood. They can only bring a gaffer and sometimes a best boy. As you go through my stories you may wonder why, when a movie I was working on went to film in New York or Chicago, I did not go with them. That is why.

Paper Moon – The Cast

Ryan ONeal

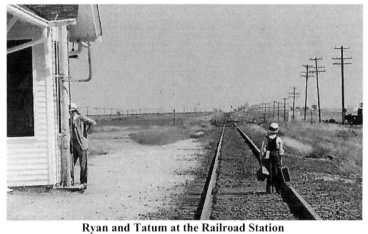

Ryan and Tatum at the Railroad Station

41

Tatum

Tatum Chained

The Drop Off

The Escape

John Hillerman

Paper Moon – Location Shots

The Picnic

The Last Shot

The Cast & Crew Hotel

FREEBIE AND THE BEAN (1973)

Starring:	Alan Arkin, James Caan, Valerie Harper, Loretta Swit, Jack Kruschen, Paul Koslo, Alex Rocco
Director:	Richard Rush
Cinematographer:	Laszlo Kovacs
Lighting Gaffer:	Aggie Aguilar
Best Boy:	Paul Caven

We filmed *Freebie and the Bean* in San Francisco from March through May 1973. This was the first film that Aggie hired me as his best boy. It was a great honor for me and the beginning of a long and wonderful relationship.

I never laughed more on a movie set in my life than I did on the set of *Freebie and the Bean*. Watching Alan Arkin and Jimmy Caan work together was unbelievably funny. The funniest scene was when the two detectives were called on the carpet in the DA's office. Alex Rocco did an outstanding job as the DA in this scene. When we did the shot where Alan and Jimmy are sitting there trying to sell their story to the DA, the interaction between Alan and Jimmy was so hysterical the crew could not contain their laughter. They had to clear the set because we could not keep from laughing and ruining takes.

We had some unique locations on this film. In one of the early scenes, the duo rides up a construction elevator to the 40th floor of a building under construction. In the process of questioning a suspect, they back him (and all of us) onto the arm of a construction crane. With three actors in front of the camera and 10 or 15 of us behind the camera holding cameras, lights, scripts and each other, the crane started to rotate out over the edge of the building. We were all trying to hold on to something, including our stomachs, while the crane had us perched 400 feet above the streets of San Francisco. I tried not to look down, but it was hard not to. I am not really afraid of heights, but this put my stomach in my throat. The scene was not over fast enough for me!

I really liked the interplay between Alan and Jimmy, but this show was all about stunts. I have never seen so many stunt people. You know when you see a scene where a person or a car or a motorcycle is going through a crowd and you see all kinds of people flying? Well not only is the driver a stunt person, but all the people flying and most of the rest of the immediate crowd are all stunt people who know exactly how to respond during the stunt. We hired a lot of extras but anyone close to where the stunts happen were all stunt people.

We had a joke we shared about stunt people, "Do you know how many stuntmen it takes to change a light bulb?" "No, how many stuntmen does it take to change a light bulb?" "Six; one to change the light bulb and five to tell him how bitchin' he did it." Just kidding, some of my best friends are stunt people.

The stunt people all joke about us "juicers" too. We all joke with each other, but on the set, we are all family. We have nicknames for each other. The people who hang out with the stunt people we call "stunt puppies." Lighting crew members were called "juicers" or "sparkies." We called costumers "rag pickers." The camera crew were "camera geeks." We called the sound crew "sound fairies" because their microphone booms hover over the set. The make-up and hair department were called the "glamour squad." The script girl, who was in charge of continuity and making sure that the actors did the same thing in take two as they did in take one, we called "Miss Match." Then when we were ready for the actors to come to the set, we would say "bring in the meat." Don't tell the actors, OK?

There were some great stunts in this show. Jimmy Nickerson was Jimmy Caan's stunt double. He did a great stunt where the principal car jumps a moving railroad flat car. The timing had to be perfect, and it worked great.

There was a stunt where a whisky truck turns over and slides towards the camera. It slid, on its side, within a couple of feet of the camera (not in the plan). The camera crew had to run for their lives, but they left the camera rolling. It ended up being a great looking shot.

There was a stunt where Jimmy and Alan's police car accidently flies off the freeway and into an apartment building. The freeway we filmed that on was the Embarcadero Freeway which was later irreparably damaged during the Loma Prieta earthquake in 1989. The car was catapulted (with dummies in it) off the freeway into a vacant lot. The apartment building was matted in later. The interior part of the scene was filmed on stage, and the special effects crew duplicated the crash by rolling the car down a track and through a break-away wall of the apartment set.

Another great stunt sequence was when Jimmy grabs a motorcycle to chase the bad guy. Mike Bast, the renowned Speedway champion, was Jimmy's stunt double for this scene and did the motorcycle stunts. He did some incredible stuff. He rode over the tops of cars going from car to car. He went up and down stairs, a lot of it on one wheel. Amazing!

Freebie and the Bean - The Lighting Team

Aggie Aguilar,
Laszlo Kovacs & Joe Thibo

Paul Caven & Aggie Aguilar

Freebie and the Bean - The Cast

Jimmy Caan

Alan Arkin

Alan Arkin & Jimmy Caan

Jimmy Caan on the Bike

47

Freebie and the Bean – The Stunts

Mike Bast Motorcycle Stunt 1

Mike Bast Motorcycle Stunt 2

Jimmy Nickerson Railroad Jump

HUCKLEBERRY FINN A Musical Adaptation (1973)

Starring: Jeff East, Paul Winfield, Harvey Korman, David Wayne

Director: J. Lee Thompson

Cinematographer: Laszlo Kovacs

Lighting Gaffer: Aggie Aguilar

Best Boy: Paul Caven

We filmed in Nauvoo, Illinois, and Natchez, Mississippi, from June to August of 1973. This was a movie that had a good director, a "maestro" for a cinematographer, the best gaffer in Hollywood with the best crew, mostly great actors, and a story that is timeless. What went wrong? For some reason they decided to make it a musical. It probably sounded like a great idea in the production meeting. The Production Company (Readers Digest) was coming off the heels of a fairly successful musical production of *Tom Sawyer.* They hired the famous Sherman brothers again to write this score, and there were a couple of good songs, one in particular by Roberta Flack, but the movie just did not sell.

J. Lee Thompson was a very good director. He was English, so he had that British formality, but he had a pretty good sense of humor. He also had an obsessive-compulsive tick. He would tear little pieces of paper out of his script and twirl them between his thumb and forefinger while he watched the scene until the piece of paper was formed into something that resembled a small dart. He would then throw that one away and tear off another piece and start the process all over again. We bought him a small tablet of paper that was perforated into strips just the right size. He got a real kick out of it and finished the whole tablet by the end of the show.

Laszlo and Aggie had their challenges on this film—not only some very rough locations on the Mississippi River, but also having to compromise their photographic sensibilities. The producers did not want to shoot at night, so we had to shoot many of the night exterior scenes in what is called "day for night." This is an old trick that was

PAUL CAVEN

used in the old TV westerns and low budget horror films where they would shoot during the day and try to make it look like night. The problem is if you happen to see the sky, you know it is not night. The only thing it saves is time and money... photographically it sucks.

The show had an inauspicious start. We flew into Chicago O'Hare Airport and then changed to several small charter planes to fly the crew to Fort Madison, Iowa, which was just across the Mississippi river from where we would be shooting in Nauvoo, Illinois. But, just as we were about to take off, they closed the main runway due to severe thunderstorms. Our flyboy said "No problem we can still take off, it's just the big planes that can't take off, trust me." Off we go into the wild, not so blue, yonder in an armada of little eight-man Cessnas. There were lightning bolts flashing all around us and the thunder was deafening. I was sitting in the co-pilot seat and was scanning the control panel when I saw the altimeter suddenly drop 600 feet. We did not go down nose first; we went down flat... 600 feet boom! I was a smoker at the time and my cigarette pack and lighter came flying up out of my shirt pocket, and my stomach was in my mouth. After an eight-man collective gasp, "Sky King" got us back up and eventually above the clouds, but not entirely out of the storm. When, by the grace of God, we got to our hotel in Fort Madison, Iowa, we found out that they were under a tornado watch. The guy at the desk said the best places to go during a tornado are either the bathroom in your room where there are no windows, or the hotel bar which also had no windows. So where do you suppose we all "hunkered down"?

The next crisis happened when the lovely ladies of the Fort Madison chapter of the DAR wanted to throw a little welcoming party for us. Apparently, they had never read Mark Twain's book because they seemed surprised to find out that we had a black person in the cast, not to mention some members of the crew. They said that all the white people were welcome, but they had never allowed a black person in their hall before, and they were not about to change that now. I hope they had a nice party, none of us showed up.

We filmed across the Mississippi River from Fort Madison, Iowa, in nearby Nauvoo, Illinois. There are more than 30 historical sites and buildings dating from 1839 to 1846 in Nauvoo. We filmed there for several days.

We then flew down to Natchez, Mississippi. The majority of the movie was filmed there. All the riverboat scenes and a lot of the street scenes were filmed in riverfront area called "Natchez under the hill." We hired a lot of local extras. It was hot and humid, and all the women had to wear long, full, period dresses. We had several women pass out from the heat. It was hot!!!

I have a couple of pictures of me operating an arc lamp perched on a Chapman camera crane. The Chapman crane is a unique piece of equipment. It is primarily for the camera. It allows the camera to be raised up high. The boom arm is what makes it unique. The arm is filled with mercury. The crane operator can pump the mercury to the opposite end of the boom from the camera in order to create enough ballast to offset the weight of the camera and everything that goes with it. Therefore, it helps to attempt to limit the amount of weight being added. In this instance, on the crane there was not only the usual camera, camera operator and camera focus puller, but also the weight of the arc light plus the arc operator. So, the crane operator had to pump enough mercury to the other end of the boom to balance it all out. There is not much that can be done about the weight of the camera, the camera operator, the focus puller or the weight of the arc lamp. The only real variable in this equation is the weight of the arc lamp operator, so it is critical that the smallest person on the lighting crew be on the crane arm and operate the lamp. As it turned out, believe it or not, I was the smallest man on my crew. So, even though I was the best boy and the best boy usually does not operate lamps, I had no other choice than to do it myself. Let me assure you, it is not as much fun as it looks.

This film had a pretty good cast. Jeff East, at the age of 17, did very well for an actor of his age. Paul Winfield was a distinguished actor. He was a kind, gentle soul, and he did a wonderful job playing "Nigger Jim". However, bigotry reared its ugly head once again in Natchez, Mississippi. The local police claimed that they intercepted a package addressed to Paul Winfield's hotel room that contained marijuana. The charge was totally false and obviously targeted. When the charges were thrown out, the local police decided if they could not get the black guy, maybe they could get some of them rich Hollywood degenerates. Word came out to the set that the police were about to start searching rooms at the hotel. All of a sudden half the crew left the set and ran back to the hotel where there was a synchronized flushing.

Working with Harvey Korman and David Wayne was a blast! These two guys provided non-stop entertainment. They clowned around on the set all the time. One picture I took is of David standing on the set while Harvey bends over behind him and picks up the tails of David's jacket as if it were an old-time camera he was looking into. They kept us all in stitches. David was one of the good guys. He would hang out with the crew at night in the hotel bar and was the life of the party.

Some actors today are trapped by the digital age. They cannot let loose like that anymore without 100 paparazzi flashing photos. On some shows they even banned personal cameras on the set because they were afraid the crew would sell photos to TMZ. You may notice as I tell my tale chronologically that the on-set photos become fewer and fewer as time goes on.

Aggie and I were in the movie as extras. We worked in a scene with Harvey where he is pretending to present a Shakespeare play to all the men in town. The entire lighting crew was standing in the back row of the room. I am the guy wearing an old top hat. Aggie is two guys to my left wearing old overalls and a big round hat.

Huckleberry Finn - The Cast

Paul Winfield

Harvey Korman

David Wayne

Jeff East

David Wayne and Harvey Korman

Huckleberry Finn - The Extras

The Extras

Paul Caven & Aggie Aguilar

54

Huckleberry Finn – The Crew At Work

Paul Caven on Camera Crane 1

Paul Caven on Camera Crane 2

On the Set

Camera Barge to Shoot Raft Scene

J. Lee Thompson
Receiving his own Tripod
(note the little strip of paper in his hand)

55

Huckleberry Finn – Location Shots

Harvey Korman, David Wayne, Paul Winfield, Jeff East

The Arrival

The Raft

AT LONG LAST LOVE (1973)

Starring:	Burt Reynolds, Cybill Shepherd, Madeline Kahn, John Hillerman, Eileen Brennan, Duilio Del Prete
Director:	Peter Bogdanovich
Cinematographer:	Laszlo Kovacs
Lighting Gaffer:	Aggie Aguilar

This was my third picture with Peter Bogdonavich as well as with some of his usual suspects, Madeline Kahn and John Hillerman, and my second picture with Burt Reynolds. We filmed around the Los Angeles area from August through October 1973. We filmed at the Huntington Library and Lacy Park in the Pasadena area. The interior sets were at 20th Century Fox Studio.

For most critics *At Long Last Love* is ranked as one of the top ten worst movies ever. I disagree! Peter wrote a fun movie, with all Cole Porter music, reminiscent of the grand Golden Age musicals of the 1930s and 1940s. It was said that the storyline was loosely patterned after Noel Coward's *Private Lives.*

The first problem was that Fox Studio would not let him shoot the movie he envisioned. He wanted to shoot it in black & white which would have sold the 1930s, 1940s look (a la *Paper Moon*). The studio said "No!" So, instead, Peter had the art director design every set to be black & white. No colors on the walls, no colors in the set dressing. The costumes were all black or white. Peter got his black & white movie in spite of the studio, but, he kind of "cut off his nose to spite his face." The problem with shooting a black & white movie in color is that all the sets end up looking bland. You cannot show any gradation of color. The only things not black & white in this film are skin color and green foliage. If Peter could have filmed this movie in black & white, the sets and costumes could have been much more visually interesting.

This was the first (and probably the only) movie to record the songs live while they were being filmed. Usually, the actor (or someone with a better voice than the actor) records the songs ahead of time then the actor actually lip-syncs the song during the filming. Peter wanted to record the songs live. An original idea, but it is a lot more trouble than it is worth. There is a reason they did it the other way for all those years.

The first problem was that other than Madeline Kahn, who had a trained singing voice, none of the other main actors were professionally trained. Cybill's singing voice was marginal. Peter sometimes lets his friendships and or his love interests affect his casting decisions. He cast people who looked the part; unfortunately, they could not sing the part. My ol' buddy Burt could not carry a tune in a bucket, but he tried, and who the hell is Duilio Del Prete? The worst was a scene where Peter wanted to film one of the songs from a moving camera car while the actors drove behind in an open convertible. The actors had earwigs in to hear the music and radio mic's to record their live singing plus they had a microphone on a boom arm on the camera car to record the overall sound. It sounded awful. Anyway, the movie was panned. Fox Studio did not put any money into advertising it, and it never made any money. For his next picture, Peter went back to Columbia Studios.

At Long Last Love - The Cast and Crew

The Whole Gang

Camera Car - On the Lights: Aggie Aguilar, Paul Caven, and
Romeo Desantis Filming One of the Songs Live from a Moving Camera Car

59

DOC SAVAGE: THE MAN OF BRONZE (1974)

Starring: Ron Ely, Paul Gleason, William Lucking, Michael Miller, Eldon Quick, Darrell Zwerling, Paul Wexler

Director: Michael Anderson

Cinematographer: Fred Koenekamp

Lighting Gaffer: Gene Stout

We filmed this movie from January to April of 1974. Some was filmed in Colorado but I did not work on that. We filmed the opening scene at the beautiful, art deco Eastern Columbia Building in downtown Los Angeles. The distinctive, thirteen story, landmark building is clad in turquoise terra cotta tiles. It has a unique four-sided clock tower with a neon lit clock on each side.

We also filmed at the Harold Lloyd Green Acres Estate in Beverly Hills. Harold Lloyd was a comic superstar of his day and for years he was the highest paid actor in Hollywood. The Estate was built in 1928. It was originally 15 acres. It had a 9 hole golf course, a 900 foot canoe stream stocked with trout and bass, a 100 foot waterfall, a complete miniature cottage built for his daughter, Gloria, and the largest swimming pool in southern California.

The inside of the mansion was just as opulent. Some of us were given a tour by a caretaker. Walking in to the 44-room house was like walking into the Twilight Zone. It was like the house was frozen in time. Nothing had been changed or replaced since the 1930s. We got to see the master bedroom where his suits were still hanging in the closet. The bathroom was beautiful with black and white tile and 1930s fixtures. We saw Gloria's bedroom and the sitting room which had a huge permanent Christmas tree for his daughter. You could not even see the tree, it was so covered in ornaments. The estate was open to the public at that time. It was soon to be closed, the estate sold and the grounds were subdivided into 14 large lots, leaving only the 5 acres the mansion was on. We also filmed at Bronson Canyon in the hills above Hollywood. The Bronson Canyon and caves have been film locations since the 1920s.

This movie takes place in the 1930s. Doc Savage and his Amazing Five Adventurers find out that Doc's father, a missionary, has disappeared in the jungles of South America and feared dead. The evil Captain Seas stands in their way as they search the country of Hidalgo for Doc's father. In their travels, they discover a stash of Inca gold. This was supposed to be the first in a series of films based on the popular series of pulp novels. However, the poor showing at the box office canceled those plans. It went to DVD.

This was my first film with Fred Koenekamp and his gaffer Gene Stout. They were a team and had worked together for years. I would work with them again seven years later on *Wrong is Right.*

Doc Savage: Man of Bronze – The Crew

**Fred Koenekamp-cinematographer (on the other side of the camera),
Michael Anderson-director (hand on glasses), George Pal,
producer (foreground), Paul Caven (beside the arc),
(Photographer: Unknown)
Location: Bronson Canyon, Hollywood**

SHAMPOO (1974)

Starring:	Warren Beatty, Julie Christie, Goldie Hawn, Jack Warden, Lee Grant, Carrie Fisher
Director:	Hal Ashby
Cinematographer:	Laszlo Kovacs
Lighting Gaffer:	Aggie Aguilar

Lee Grant won the Academy Award for Best Supporting Actress in this film, and Jack Warden was nominated for the Academy Award for Best Supporting Actor. Robert Towne also was nominated for an Academy Award for Best Original Screenplay. The Film was nominated for a Golden Globe Award. Warren Beatty, Julie Christie, Goldie Hawn, and Lee Grant were also nominated for Golden Globes.

We filmed *Shampoo* in and around Los Angeles from June through August 1974. We almost lost Warren Beatty on the first day of filming. We were shooting the opening sequence where he is riding his motorcycle. Warren insisted on doing his own motorcycle riding, but I am not sure how much time he had ever spent on a motorcycle. It was obvious he was not an experienced rider. It was early in the morning and the roads were damp with dew. Warren came around a corner a little too fast and almost lost it. He was able to recover and keep going, but we all thought the show was going to end early.

We filmed a night sequence where Warren and Julie make love on the floor of a tennis room by a single light coming from an open refrigerator door. The 15-watt refrigerator light was, of course, not bright enough so, we rigged one of our 1000-watt movie lights inside the refrigerator. It was a great looking shot. We were in the middle of filming it when it came time to go to dinner. We turned off our power and went to eat. Unfortunately, we forgot that our refrigerator light was plugged into the house power, not our power. When we got back to work an hour later and opened the refrigerator door, we realized we did not turn off our 1000-watt light in this rented refrigerator, the inside of which now looked like "The Fantastic Caverns." The plastic

63

was all melted and dripping from the top like so many stalactites. The plastic sides were drooping like some kind of big fat beer belly. Aggie and I were laughing and desperately trying to remold the warm plastic when Warren walked in to see what happened. He just shook his head and walked out. OOOPS!!! Luckily for us they did not see inside the refrigerator during the shot; all they saw was the light coming out of it, so we were able to keep shooting.

As they were filming one of the interior scenes in Julie's character's house, we were all sitting outside on the patio while they shot inside. I was fiddling with one of our switches that controlled the lights for the shot inside. I was cleaning it up, pulling old tape off it when I mistakenly turned the switch off and turned off all the lights inside during the filming. Warren came storming out looking for blood, "What happened! Who did that?" he bellowed. I quickly said, "It's OK Warren, I found the problem and I took care of it. We're good to go now." He took a quick look around to see if anyone had a smirk on their face; seeing none he turned and went back in the house. Sometimes it pays to be able to think on the fly.

The big party scene was filmed at a mansion that was for sale in the Hombly Hills area of Beverly Hills. It took almost two weeks, working from sun-down to sun-up, to shoot the sequence. They hired a whole bunch of extras, and it was basically a two-week party! The prop department had a dilemma. They needed a lot of "joints" (of Bull Durham tobacco) rolled to use as props at the party scene. None of them knew how to do that, so "who ya gonna call?"... The Juicers!!! We must have rolled hundreds and hundreds of joints... most of them with Bull Durham.

On most shows, the crew picks up on a line or two from the script, and it becomes the comic line for the show. On *Shampoo,* the line was Jack Warden's character saying, "Am I right or am I right?" We would use it all the time and always got a big laugh every time.

Warren was a nice enough guy, a little vain but Carly Simon warned us about that. One of the assistant directors wore a T-shirt saying, "Carly was right". When Warren saw it he laughed out loud.

Goldie Hawn was a sweetheart, just a ball of fire. She was exactly like you saw on "Laugh In." Her giggle was contagious. Anytime she was on the set, it brought everyone's spirits up.

This was Carrie Fisher's film debut, she was almost 18 years old. Her mother, Debbie Reynolds, was reportedly not happy with the sexual frankness of her young daughter's part.

Hal Ashby was a wonderful, kind, soft-spoken, down-to-earth, excellent director. He directed *Harold and Maude, The Last Detail, Coming Home* and *Being There*. Unfortunately, he had to contend with kibitzing from Warren and Robert Towne. Robert Towne was rewriting the script while we were shooting it. Warren would question just about everything Hal would say.

For the wrap party, we all got together and bought Hal a very nice piccolo case. Instead of a piccolo inside, the juicers rolled one huge 18-inch-long "joint"... of Bull Durham, of course. Suffice it to say, the piccolo case went home with Hal empty. It was a great wrap party. Sadly, Hal, passed away in 1988 at the age of 59.

Shampoo - The Cast and Crew

The Camera Car - Shooting On the Move

The Crew on Special Assignment

Goldie Hawn's Good Wishes

BABY BLUE MARINE (1975)

Starring:	Jan Michael Vincent, Glynnis O'Connor, Katherine Helmond, Dana Elcar, Bert Remsen, Bruno Kirby, Richard Gere, Adam Arkin, Marshall Efron
Director:	John Hancock
Cinematographer:	Laszlo Kovacs
Lighting Gaffer:	Aggie Aguilar
Best Boy:	Paul Caven

We filmed some of this movie in the Los Angeles area but the majority of it was filmed in McCloud, California, and on the McCloud River in the shadow of magnificent Mount Shasta, from April through June of 1975. It is a cute little love story set in a small town during the Second World War. John Hancock does a brilliant job portraying a Norman Rockwell America from a simpler time. Laszlo's photography was spectacular. The scenery stunning! Jan Michael and Glynnis were impressive. It had a dazzling list of supporting actors—marvelous character actors like Bert Remsen, Adam Arkin, Dana Elcar, Bruno Kirby, Marshall Efron, and Richard Gere.

It is a thought-provoking story about a young man, Marion (Jan Michael Vincent) who joins the Marines during WWII but failed basic training and was sent home in a light baby blue uniform which indicates that he washed out of the Marines. He meets a real war vet (Richard Gere) in a bar who wants to go AWOL because he is afraid to be sent back. The vet mugs Marion in an alley and takes his clothes, leaving him the war vet uniform to wear.

Marion hitchhikes towards home but on the way, he stops in a small mountain town and the people, of course, think he is a war hero. A young waitress at the café invites him to stay with her family until he is ready to leave. Their relationship blossoms to love.

While he is there it is reported that three Japanese teens have escaped from a near-by internment camp. The whole town is ready to hunt them down and kill them as if they were actual Japanese soldiers. Marion is recruited to help find them. He finds one of the teens trying to escape by swimming across the river. He does not make it and is swept downstream. Marion demonstrates his true heroism by risking his own life to save the teen's life. I do not know why this movie did not do better at the box office. I thought it was a good movie.

The river scenes were filmed on the McCloud River. There was a dead tree that had fallen over across the river from one bank to the other. The crew built a walkway along the tree so they could place a camera over the center of the river. They also put a camera in a raft to film on the river.

Richard Gere had a small but pivotal part as the WWII hero vet in one scene that takes place in a bar. The bar set was built in the basement of an old building in downtown Los Angeles. It was small and cramped, not a lot of places to position our lights. Our high-intensity lights get very hot; therefore, we are always conscious of fire sprinklers. Fire sprinklers are set off by heat, not smoke. There is a little wad of wax on top of the sprinkler. If that wax melts, the sprinklers go off. When one goes off, they all go off and it is not a pretty sight.

Well, you guessed it. This little room got over-heated and right in the middle of a shot, the sprinklers in this 80-year-old building went off. The water in the lines was so old, however, that the scum in the water lines mercifully clogged some of the sprinklers. The water that did come out was so smelly, it was nauseating. The extras were all soaked. The set was soaked. We were soaked. Finally, the LA Fire Department came and was able to pump the water out. Well, the show must go on, so we cleaned up the set as best we could, changed the extras' costumes and kept on shooting. There was not much we could do about our clothes, so we had to just spend the rest of the day in smelly clothes.

Baby Blue Marine - The Cast

Glynnis O'Connor & Jan Michael Vincent

Jan Michael Vincent & Michael Narita

Glynnis O'Connor, Jan Michael Vincent and Mt. Shasta

Baby Blue Marine – Our Leaders

Director John Hancock

Laszlo Kovacs

69

Baby Blue Marine - The Crew on Location

Filming on the McCloud River

Filming the rapids from a raft

Filming from a well-placed log

THE ENTERTAINER (1975)

Starring:	Jack Lemmon, Ray Bolger, Sada Thompson, Tyne Daly and Annette O'Toole
Director:	Donald Wrye
Cinematographer:	James Crabe

This was a made for TV movie that we filmed in the summer of 1975 in the Los Angeles area and in the beach community of Santa Cruz, California. This film had a phenomenal cast and it was a thrill to work with such legends as Jack Lemmon and Ray Bolger. I would work with them both again later. One day when Ray Bolger was on his way to the set, he passed a group of people watching us shoot. Ray, the consummate entertainer, broke into a little "scarecrow" song and dance for the people. It was wonderful to see. Sada Thompson and Tyne Daly were also incredible. Annette O'Toole was sweet and did an amazing job.

This show was nominated for five Emmys. Nominated were: Jack Lemmon, Ray Bolger, Sada Thompson, the writer of the screenplay Elliot Baker, and the cinematographer James Crabe. This was a musical, but most of the music was in the stage acts. There was some fantastic original music written by a young Marvin Hamlisch. The cinematographer, Jimmy Crabe, was a wonderful person, kind, gentle, with a fantastic sense of humor. He was a wonderful cinematographer with a crisp clean look. Jimmy was an expert on the great Hollywood musicals of the 1930s and 1940s. If you mentioned a musical, he would break into a song and dance from that musical. He could do them all. I would work with Jimmy a few more times, but he unfortunately passed away in 1989 at the age of 57.

This film was a re-make of the 1960 film by the same name starring Laurence Olivier, about an aging vaudeville performer, played by Jack Lemmon who sees his career and life crumble in front of him until he meets a young girl played by Annette O'Toole, who makes him feel young again. In one scene, they go to the Santa Cruz Wharf Amusement Park which has a world-famous wooden rollercoaster called The Giant Dipper. It was built in 1924 and is still in use today. We were to film Jack and Annette while riding on the rollercoaster. The problem was, to do that the cameraman, the director and some dummy with a light had to be in the car in front of them, facing backwards. Well, who do you think got picked to ride the rollercoaster holding a light facing backwards? "Hey kid, come'er and hold this light and make sure you keep it on the actors…oh, and hold on." So, the camera operator, the director and I have the distinction of being the only idiots ever to ride the Santa Cruz rollercoaster facing backwards!

Toward the end of the show we were running a little behind schedule, so we had to check out of the Holiday Inn and move to another hotel. Unfortunately, for the Company, the only available rooms were in the most expensive hotel in town. It was on the beach with all the amenities, beach volleyball courts and beach chairs with umbrellas lined up all in a row. The plan was to check in after work that night.

As we were wrapping up from the day's work, I was accidentally cracked over the head by one of the guys on the crew carrying a lamp stand. As you may know, head wounds bleed a lot. By the time they got me to the hospital, I had blood running down my face into my beard and down the front of my T-shirt. In the emergency room they had to shave an area of my hair to allow for seven stitches, but they did not clean me up at all. Of course, by the time I got to the hotel everyone else had already checked in. I walk in the lobby of this ritzy hotel with a big bald spot on my head, blood streaking through my hair, blood clotted in my beard and dried blood down the front of my T-shirt. I walk up to the front desk. "May I help you?" The desk clerk asked in a condescending tone. "Hello, I'd like to check in," I said. The desk clerk, trying not to look horrified, said, "Do you have a reservation sir?" "Yes, I'm with the movie company." "Oh, more movie people, I should have known." I have never been checked in as fast as I was that night. Hurray for Hollywood!

The Entertainer – The Cast and Crew

Jack Lemmon & Annette O'Toole

Paul Caven, Ray Bolger, Grip, Gene Kearney (Key Grip)

73

Donald Wrye (Director), Paul Caven, Ronald Schwary (1st Asst. Director)

1 **Ray Bolger's Good Wishes**

HARRY AND WALTER GO TO NEW YORK (1975)

Starring: James Caan, Elliot Gould, Michael Caine and
                         Diane Keaton

Director: Mark Rydell

Cinematographer: Laszlo Kovacs

Lighting Gaffer: Aggie Aguilar

Best Boy: Paul Caven

Another show with Jimmy Caan, another sore jaw from laughing too much! Between Jimmy Caan and Elliot Gould, it was non-stop laughs. They play two con men that have a traveling stage act where they do a song and dance routine and then try to soak the audience with a phony fortune teller act. Yes, they sing and dance. Jimmy and Elliot do a great job in this film. It had an impressive cast.

It was great working with Michael Caine; he is a class act. Michael's character, Adam Worth, was a real person and one of the most notorious criminals of the 19th Century. Diane Keaton was marvelous. I would work with her again at the end of my career on *Because I Said So.*

I also got to work with my old buddy Bert Remsen again. I worked with him on *Baby Blue Marine.* Bert was great, always friendly and easy to get along with. He started out working as a talent agent then, I guess, decided to do the job himself. There were a lot of great character actors in this show like, Charles Durning, Jack Gilford, Dennis Dugan, Carol Kane, Burt Young, Jack O'Halloran and Lesley Ann Warren. I would work with Lesley Ann again on another movie.

We filmed from August to October of 1975. All the interior scenes were filmed on stage at Warner Brothers Studio. Some of the New York scenes were filmed on the old *Hello Dolly* set that was still standing on the Twentieth Century Fox back lot. The prison and some of the other exteriors were filmed in and around Mansfield, Ohio.

The prison was a working prison. We filmed there for weeks.

Nothing will scare you straight faster than spending a couple of weeks in prison. One time as I was passing through the visitor center, I saw one prisoner visiting with his wife and nine-year-old daughter. They were blowing out the candles on a birthday cake that said "Happy 9th Birthday." It broke my heart. Something else that was heart wrenching was seeing the prison cemetery. It was just outside the walls and the first thing you notice is that there are no names on the headstones, only numbers... the final punishment.

The prison did not have any extra guards to assign to us, so they assigned a few trustees to help us. Most of the trustees were lifers and, thereby, respected and feared by their peers. They helped us with crowd control and getting from one place to another. I would work at that prison again on another show 14 years later and some of those same trustees were still there.

Not everyone was thrilled about us being there. The prisoners did not like their schedule being disrupted. When we were shooting out in the yard, they were not allowed out. When we were shooting in the cellblocks, they were not allowed in. One day it all came to a head and the prisoners started a small riot. That, of course, triggered a lockdown... nobody in and nobody out. Unfortunately, we were in. They told us, "If you hear a gunshot, hit the ground because anyone standing or running would be shot!" It took most of the day but the prisoners came up with a list of demands and some of them concerned us. The warden rearranged some of their scheduling and calmed everything down and eventually we were able to leave.

This movie went massively over budget and caused such a major cash crisis that Columbia Pictures nearly went out of business, until a German businessman agreed to help finance the studio's other movies. After disastrous previews, Columbia Pictures cut the movie way down. It never did very well at the box office.

Harry and Walter Go To New York – The Cast

Michael Caine
(Photo Credit: Black & White Production
Still Photo by Dave Friedman Company, Still
Photographer)

Jimmy Caan
(Photo Credit: Black & White Production
Still Photo by Dave Friedman Company, Still
Photographer)

Diane Keaton
(Photo Credit: Black & White Production
Still Photo by Dave Friedman Company, Still
Photographer)

Elliot Gould
(Photo Credit: Black & White Production
Still Photo by Dave Friedman Company, Still
Photographer)

Harry and Walter Go To New York – The Cast and Crew in Action

Jimmy Caan & Elliott Gould

Jimmy Caan

Harry and Walter Go To New York –
The Cast and Crew in Action (con't)

Jimmy Caan, Laszlo Kovacs, Mark Rydell

While most of the attention is focused on the stars and the action, production personnel go unnoticed as they move lights, cameras, sound equipment and other items from scene to scene.

Paul Caven Makes the Newspaper

FRIENDLY PERSUASION (1975)

Starring: Richard Kiley, Shirley Knight, Michael O'Keefe

Director: Joseph Sargent

Cinematographer: Mario Tosi

Lighting Gaffer: Joe Pender

This movie was a TV remake of the classic 1956 film by the same name starring Gary Cooper and Dorothy McQuire. We filmed this show at a home in rural Missouri in the Blue Springs area and at a historical 1855 pioneer site called Missouri Town from October through November of 1975. It had a pretty good cast, but it is hard to beat the original classic with Gary Cooper.

Richard Kiley was an accomplished Broadway actor and very friendly. Shirley Knight was also an accomplished actress and was great in this part. The director, Joseph Sargent, had an impressive résumé. He had just finished *The Taking of Pelham One Two Three*. Mario Tosi was Italian, and a fine cameraman with a sensitive eye for color and light. Joe Pender was Mario's gaffer. Joe had worked with us on *Shampoo,* so when he got this gaffing job, he called me. That's how it works in this business a lot of times. Just like in the old days, you hire people you know and have worked with. I worked with Joe and Mario one more time on the award-winning TV movie *Sybil*.

Friendly Persuasion – The Cast and and Crew

Shirley Knight & Michael O'Keefe

Joseph Sargent, Richard Kiley, Mario Tosi

Joe Pender

Joseph Sargent

Mario Tosi

Paul Caven & Richard Kiley

81

PAUL CAVEN

SYBIL (1976)

Starring: Joanne Woodward, Sally Field

Director: Daniel Petrie

Cinematographer: Mario Tosi

Lighting Gaffer: Joe Pender

This was a TV movie of the week that we filmed in February and March 1976 at Warner Brothers Studio. They also filmed in New York, however, I did not work on that part. It is based on the true story of a young woman named Sybil, played by Sally Field, who is diagnosed as suffering from multiple personalities as a result of severe abuse at the hands of her mother. Sybil's sixteen personalities were brought out by her psychiatrist, played by Joanne Woodward.

Both Sally Field and Joanne Woodward did incredible work on this show. Sybil was an extraordinarily difficult part and Sally Field gave an astonishing performance. The show won six awards and was nominated for five more. Sally Field won a Prime Time Emmy and Joanne Woodward was nominated for a Prime Time Emmy. Mario Tosi was also nominated for a Prime Time Emmy for cinematography.

Production Company Thank You Letter

NICKELODEON (1976)

Starring:	Ryan O'Neal, Burt Reynolds, Tatum O'Neal, Brian Keith, Stella Stevens, John Ritter and Jane Hitchcock
Director:	Peter Bogdanovich
Cinematographer:	Laszlo Kovacs
Lighting Gaffer:	Aggie Aguilar
Best Boy:	Paul Caven (my first screen credit)

We filmed this movie at Warner Brothers Studio and in Modesto, California, from March to May 1976.

This was my fourth picture with Peter. I liked this movie but the critics did not. It was another Peter Bogdanovich slapstick comedy ala *What's Up Doc.* He even has a suitcase mix-up gag just like in *What's Up Doc.*

What I like about the film is the underlying story line about the turbulent birth of the Hollywood movie industry and the "Edison Patent Wars." Thomas Edison had several patents for the movie camera and movie projectors. In 1908 he and several other inventors created the Motion Picture Patent Company. The member companies legally monopolized the business, and demanded licensing fees from all film producers, distributors, and exhibitors. A January 1909 deadline was set for all companies to comply with the license. By February, unlicensed outlaws, who referred to themselves as *independents,* protested the trust and carried on business without submitting to the Edison monopoly.

In the summer of 1909 in Chicago, the independent movement was in full swing, with producers and theater owners using illegal equipment and imported film stock to create their own underground market. To avoid the Trust some producers decided to move their operation to southern California. Carl Laemmle (Independent Motion Picture Company or IMP), Harry E. Aitken (Majestic Films), Adolph Zukor (Famous Players), and William Fox were among the

83

pioneering independents who protested the Trust, and thereby laid the foundation for the Hollywood studios. Furthermore, by moving their studios out west, the outlaws were not only capitalizing on California's optimal year-round outdoor shooting conditions, they were also pioneering a division between the east-coast business headquarters and the west-coast production operation that would become another trademark of the Hollywood studio system.

Unfortunately, The Patent Company did not take all of this lying down. They sent enforcers to Hollywood to try to break-up the independents. In October 1915, the courts determined that the Patents Company acted as a monopoly in restraint of trade, and later ordered it dismantled. This is the backdrop for *Nickelodeon*.

Peter once again assembled the usual suspects: Ryan and Tatum O'Neal and Burt Reynolds, as well as using Griffin O'Neal again as another bicycle delivery boy... type casting! Even my old buddy Frank Marshall had a small part as Dinsdale's assistant. Brian Keith, who plays the producer Dinsdale, was, of course, an old pro, as was Stella Stevens (although not so old). John Ritter was fun to work with. He was raised in the business watching his father, Tex Ritter, so he knew the importance of the crew. This was the first and last movie for Jane Hitchcock. She was very nice but she was primarily a dancer and only worked on one other TV show later. Harry Carey Jr., James Best, John Chappell and Jack Verbois play the motley movie crew.

Peter, like many directors, likes to give actors some kind of "business" to deal with, something to add to the depth of their character. In this picture he had Jack's character have a speech impediment, he stutters. I have a speech impediment, I stutter. Remember this was my 4th picture with Peter. Peter never told me, but I have a feeling that he patterned that movie crew character after me. The only other time he did that in any of his movies was later on in another show I worked with him on, *Mask*. I'm just sayin'.

There is a scene towards the end of the movie where some Patent Company thugs one night burn down the house containing our hero's film lab. The plan was to show the initial explosion and fire provided by the special effects crew, then cut. The fire department would then put out any little flare-ups. We would wrap our lights out and the special effects crew would wrap all their gas lines out then leave. Overnight the fire department would finish burning the building. We would come back the next day to film the next part of the scene, with the house burned out.

That was the plan. That is not what happened. After we started rolling, Peter decided he wanted to keep shooting and see more of the fire. The problem was, of course, we had our lights inside and we certainly did not want them to burn up with the rest of the building. So, as soon as Peter cut, I cut the power to our lights and the effects crew turned their gas lines off. I lead a couple of my crew as we ran into the burning building to grab our lights. Even though the gas lines were off, the room our lights were in was fully engulfed in flame. There was fire on all four walls, it was hotter than hell and the room was quickly filling with smoke. We grabbed our lights and cable and ran out. I never should have done that. I would never have forgiven myself if one of my guys would have gotten hurt and I swore I would never again put any of my crew in that kind of peril. It's only a movie!

As I said, this was a slapstick comedy, so there were plenty of stunts. Hal Needham was the stunt coordinator and Burt's stunt double. During the production, Hal decided to try to quit smoking. The program he went through had negative, anti-smoking posters on the walls as part of their treatment. They also used pro-smoking advertising posters as talking points against smoking. He told us one of the pro-smoking posters they used was a poster with the "Marlboro Man" on a horse with a cigarette in his mouth. The problem was the cowboy in the picture was Hal Needham. Understandably that program did not work for Hal.

Hal was a legendary pioneer for the modern stuntman. He understood how best to choreograph a stunt so as to get the maximum camera coverage. He lined up a stunt for this film that was going to be photographically perfect but it almost went horribly wrong.

The stunt involved Hal (as Burt) and Julie Johnson (as Jane Hitchcock's character). Julie was a veteran stunt woman. She and a handful of talented, knowledgeable women were some of the first women to be admitted in to the Stuntmen's Association. Many years later she would become the first woman stunt coordinator. The way the scene was written, it shows Hal in a hot air balloon basket about to lift off when Julie accidently finds herself caught by the ankle in one of the balloon's mooring ropes. As the balloon goes up, we see Julie hanging by one of her ankles ten feet below the basket.

Hal worked with the special effects crew to rig the hot air balloon. We only needed to see the balloon go up about 100 feet and then we would cut. So, they tethered the balloon to the ground with 4 cables that were out of the shot and would only allow the balloon to rise 100 feet. They also rigged Julie to the gondola by a cable that was on a winch, allowing her to be suspended 10 feet below, and then be able to be winched back up into the basket. As we rolled the cameras the stunt was going fine. You see Hal in the gondola, and you see Julie hanging from the gondola in her bloomers with her dress hanging over her head. As they got to the 100-foot mark, they encountered an unforeseen problem. The wind speed was much higher at 100 feet than it was on the ground. The strong wind broke a couple of the cables holding the balloon and it started to whip Julie around uncontrollably. She did not know what had happened; her dress was hanging over her eyes. We had already cut so Hal immediately started winching Julie back up to safety. The special effects crew was then able to limp the balloon back down to the ground with the remaining cables. It was a great shot and a good stunt but it could have been a disaster.

There were a bunch of sayings the crew picked up on in this movie. Like when John Ritter, playing the cameraman, tries to reassure Ryan, who is playing the reluctant rookie director in the movie, by saying, "Don't worry, any jerk can direct." Or when Burt, playing the lead actor in the movie, complains about his costume saying that, "Nobody can act in these socks." Or when the Indian extras they hire for the movie refuse to work on their mountainside set citing religious objections saying, "No go devil mountain." The crew picked up on all of these lines and would evoke them at appropriate moments.

There was another quote, however, that I loved the most. At the end of the movie, even though everything has gone bad, they realize that they must continue to be part of this amazing new medium. Brian Keith, the flamboyant producer, comes to the realization that, "Movies are a language that everybody understands like music for the eyes and, if you're good, if you're really good, then maybe what you're doing is giving them little tiny pieces of time that they never forget." Amen!!!

Nickelodeon – The Cast

Jane Hitchcock and Burt Reynolds

Jane Hitchcock, Burt Reynolds, Stella Stevens

Burt Reynolds" Good Wishes

Tatum O'Neal's Good Wishes

Ryan O'Neal and Burt Reynolds

87

Nickelodeon – The Crew

Nickelodeon Crew Photo – Waiting on Ryan
(Photo by Bruce McBroom (Company Still Photographer)

Aggie Aguilar

Nickelodeon – The Cast and Crew in Action

The Balloon and the Train

Rigging for the Balloon Shots

**Jane Hitchcock & Burt Reynolds
About to Hit the Water Tower**

**Burt Reynolds & Jane Hitchcock
Hit the Water Tower**

Burt Reynolds & Jane Hitchcock Land on the Train

Nickelodeon – The Cast and Crew in Action

Ryan O'Neal & Hal Needham
Rehearse The Fight

Ryan O'Neal's Pants Fall Down
During The Fight

Ryan O'Neal Directing Burt Reynolds

Ryan O'Neal Fixing Burt Reynolds' Hat

Ryan O'Neal in Burt Reynolds' Hat

Company Crew Picture

ONE ON ONE (1976)

Starring:	Robby Benson, Annette O'Toole, G.D. Spradlin, Gail Strickland, Melanie Griffith
Director:	Lamont Johnson
Cinematographer:	Donald Morgan
Lighting Gaffer:	Don Nygren

This production was filmed in part in Colorado but I joined them when they came back to Los Angeles. We filmed in May and June of 1976, around the Los Angeles area, at Warner Bros. Studio and at the University of California at Santa Barbara.

The story is about a small town High School basketball star, Henry Steele, played by Robby Benson, who gets a basketball scholarship to a big city university. Henry becomes overwhelmed by the demands on his time, the big business aspect of college sports and the fact that he never really learned to read. They assign a pretty senior student Janet Hays, played by Annette O'Toole, to tutor him. Her intellect and strength give Henry the power to stand up to the coach who is attempting to rescind Henry's scholarship.

This was my first film with Don Nygren. The studio best boy was Leroy Hershkowitz. Leroy had just worked for me and Aggie on *Nickelodeon* so when he started this movie he called me. Also on the crew was Don's friend John "Tuna" Autonovich. I would work with Don and Tuna on their next show, *Murder at the World Series.* This is the only time I worked with the cameraman, Don Morgan. He was a well-known TV Cinematographer.

I worked with Annette O'Toole the year before on, *The Entertainer.* She was very nice. Robby Benson was very nice also. He co-wrote the script with his screenwriter father Jerry Segal. Nineteen year old Melanie Griffith had a very small part in this film as a hitchhiker. A decade later she was one of the most famous actresses in Hollywood. The director, Lamont Johnson, gave himself a small part in this film; he was an actor before he started directing. He was a good TV director.

PAUL CAVEN

MURDER AT THE WORLD SERIES (1976)

Starring:	Linda Day George, Murray Hamilton, Karen Valentine, Gerald S. O'Loughlin, Michael Parks, Janet Leigh, Hugh O'Brian, Bruce Boxleitner
Director:	Andrew V. McLaglen
Cinematographer:	Richard C. Glouner
Lighting Gaffer:	Don Nygren

We filmed this TV movie in July of 1976 in Houston, Texas. It was a grueling schedule. We worked 21 days straight without a day off in the oppressive humid heat of Houston in July. We filmed a few locations around Houston but the majority of the filming was done in the Houston Astrodome.

This was the only time I worked with Richard Glouner. Dick was a good TV cameraman. He had a great personality and a wonderful sense of humor. This was the second film I did with Don Nygren and his best boy, John Autonovich. I had just worked with them earlier that year on a movie called *One On One*.

The story is about a troubled young man, Cisco, played by Bruce Boxleitner, who tries out for the Houston Astros and is rejected. He plots to get revenge with a series of kidnappings and bombings.

It had an all-star cast. They were all well-known TV actors. I would work with Bruce Boxleitner three years later on *The Baltimore Bullet*. Janet Leigh had her daughter Jamie Leigh Curtis on the payroll as a dialog coach. She was about 18 or 19 years old at the time. Jamie Leigh was a cute, bubbly, sweet young girl. She was the sweetheart of the crew. Everybody loved her. She would later go by Jamie Lee Curtis.

They hired several Houston Astros players and minor league players to work as extras. They also used major league umpires and the Astros announcer Bob Allen as well as Dick Enberg.

92

Murder At the World Series – The Cast

Cynthia Avila, Karen Valentine, Gerald O'Loughlin

The Astros Players

Audience with Actors in Front Row

Murder At the World Series – The Crew, Location and Van Stunt

Dick Glouner

Don Nygren & John Autonovich

The Production Equipment Truck

Exploding Van

CASEY'S SHADOW (1976)

Starring:	Walter Matthau, Alexis Smith, Robert Webber, Murray Hamilton, Steve Burns, and Michael Hershewe
Director:	Martin Ritt
Cinematographer:	John Alonzo
Lighting Gaffer:	James Plannette

This is a cute little "boy and his horse" movie written by the wonderfully sensitive screenwriter Carol Sobieski. I would work on another show she wrote called, *The Toy* a few years later. The director Marty Ritt was a very talented director and a nice person. This was my first film with Jim Plannette and John Alonzo. I would work with both of them again on other films.

This movie had a veteran cast headed by Walter Matthau. Walter was a real friendly guy. As you may expect, he was also quite the gambler. He owned race horses and was an avid poker player. Almost every weekend on location he would host a big poker game with some of the guys on the crew. He did not always win, but he and the guys really had a great time. He said something very profound one time about gambling. He stated that most real gamblers almost prefer losing to winning. He explained that the feelings associated with losing last longer than the feeling associated with winning. I guess that is true, but I prefer winning.

Another interesting fact about Walter was that he could not drive. Because he lived in New York City, he never needed to drive. It was painfully obvious in the opening scene when he tried to drive the old stick shift pickup truck during the shot. First, he could not get it started (which became a running gag throughout the show), then when he did get it started, he lunged forward and then stopped and then lunged forward again, and then stalled. After he got it started again, he went on to drive rather poorly. We all just stayed out of his way. He got better at it with more practice.

We filmed in Ruidoso, New Mexico, and Lafayette, Louisiana, from August to October of 1976. All of the race footage was done in

Ruidoso at Ruidoso Downs during the Million Dollar Futurity Stakes. It was really interesting to see the inner workings of the race horse business. We also filmed the live birth of a foal. That was incredible.

The rest of the show was filmed in Lafayette, Cajun country. Cajuns are a warm, friendly, fun-loving people who love to sing and dance and eat. This was my first experience eating Cajun food; étouffée, jambalaya, crawfish pie, filé gumbo, me-o my-o… it was wonderful! Almost every weekend we would be invited to a local Cajun cookout. There was always live music and plenty of crawfish. They would eat and drink, sing and dance and eat some more. I loved it all.

John Alonzo was an excellent, hard working cinematographer and a fun person. He started his career as an actor. He was in *The Magnificent Seven*. I liked working for Jim Plannette. Jim grew up in the business, his father, Homer Plannette, was a well known gaffer. Jim's son Paul Plannette is also in the business. Jim was always calm, cool and collected. They used to call him Gentleman Jim because he was so respectful to his crew. I would work for him later on several other shows and best boy for him as well.

Casey's Shadow – The Cast and Crew

Walter Matthau

Walter Matthau & Robert Webber

Robert Webber, Walter Matthau &
Steve Burns

Michael Hershewe & Paul Caven

Walter Matthau's Good Wishes

97

THE CHEAP DETECTIVE (1977)

Starring:	Peter Falk, Ann-Margret, Eileen Brennan, Sid Caesar, Madeline Kahn, Fernando Lamas
Director:	Robert Moore
Cinematographer:	John Alonzo
Lighting Gaffer:	James Plannette
Best Boy:	Paul Caven

We filmed this movie at Warner Brothers Studio from May through July of 1977. This is a classic Neil Simon script, wall to wall one liners, spoofs and visual gags. It had a blockbuster cast: Peter Falk, Ann-Margret, Eileen Brennan, Sid Caesar, Stockard Channing, James Coco, Dom DeLuise, Louise Fletcher, John Houseman, Madeline Kahn, Fernando Lamas, Marsha Mason, Phil Silvers, Abe Vigoda, Paul Williams, Nicol Williamson, Scatman Crothers, David Ogdan Stiers, and Vic Tayback.

This was my second picture with Eileen Brennan. I worked with her on *At Long Last Love.* She had a great sense of humor. I also worked with Scatman Crothers before on *King of Marvin Gardens.* This was my fourth and last picture with Madeline Kahn. She was such a great comedic actress. She had a phenomenal sense of timing. Unfortunately, her life was cut short by cancer in 1999 at the age of 57. She did an extraordinary job in this movie. Her character uses 16 names: Denise Manderley, Wanda Coleman, Gilda Dabney, Chloe LaMarr, Alma Chalmers, Alma Palmers, Vivian Purcell, Carmen Montenegro, Diane Glucksman, Mrs. Danvers, Natasha Ublenskaya, Sophie DeVega, Mary Jones, Lady Edwina Morgan St. Paul, Norma Shearer, and Barbara Stanwyck. The name used most is Mrs. Montenegro. This was my one and only film with Ann-Margret and let me say right now that Ann-Margret was the most beautiful woman I have ever seen (my wife Denise excluded). She had a natural beauty that shined through in her charming personality.

As I mentioned, this movie is full of spoofs. Ann-Margret's Jezebel Dezire is a spoof of Lauren Bacall's Marie (Slim) Browning from *To Have and Have Not*; Madeline Kahn's Mrs. Montenegro is a spoof of Mary Astor's Brigid O'Shaughnessy in *The Maltese Falcon*; John Houseman's Jasper Blubber is a spoof of Sydney Greenstreet's Kasper Gutman (The Fat Man) in *The Maltese Falcon*; Dom DeLuise's Pepe Damascus is a spoof of Peter Lorre; Fernando Lamas' Paul DuChard is a spoof of Paul Henreid's Victor Laszlo from *Casablanca*; Paul Williams' Boy is a spoof of Elisha Cook Jr.; Scatman Crothers' pianist Tinker is a spoof of Dooley Wilson's piano player Sam from *Casablanca*; Louise Fletcher's Marlene DuChard is a spoof of Ingrid Bergman's Ilsa Lund from *Casablanca* whilst Peter Falk's Lou Peckinpaugh is an amalgam spoof of two Humphrey Bogart characters, Sam Spade from *The Maltese Falcon* and Rick Blaine from *Casablanca* and is an extension of his Sam Diamond character from *Murder by Death* and his *Columbo* character from television. The name of the bar, Nix Place, is a spoof of the bar Rick's Place from *Casablanca*.

Warner Brothers prop department still had all the old light fixtures and decorations from Rick's Place allowing the art director, Charles B. Pierce, to use the original set dressing for the Nix Place set. Also, the farewell scene between Lou Peckinpaugh (Peter Falk) and Marlene DuChard (Louise Fletcher) was filmed on the same sound stage that was used for the Humphrey Bogart and Ingrid Bergman farewell in *Casablanca*.

This was my second picture with Jim Plannette and John Alonzo. I worked with them on *Casey's Shadow* as a lighting tech but Jim hired me as the best boy on this show. Many people in the business have little things that they are known for, something that sets them apart. John Alonzo was known for wearing a white terrycloth kango style cap. He would award caps to his regular camera crew or to people who distinguished themselves as being worthy. It took me two pictures but I finally earned my cap on *The Cheap Detective*.

One of the opening scenes takes place outside an old hotel in downtown Los Angeles. When we arrived on location, John Alonzo noticed that the old hotel's neon sign was not working. He wanted it to work because you can see it in the first shot. The manager of the hotel said it had not worked for many, many years. Well, when the cameraman wants something to work in the shot, it is the Best Boys' job to make it work. So, I went up to the roof to inspect the sign. It looked as if the neon and the ballasts were all still intact, but the power had been disconnected long ago. I ran some power off of our portable generators all the way up to the roof, hooked up the sign and crossed my fingers that it would still work. Low and behold the 40-year-old sign still worked. I went back to John and showed him the sign then stood there waiting to receive my terrycloth cap for performing above and beyond the call of duty. Instead, he said, "That's great but can you make it flicker?" "OH!"

Luckily in my kit I had a mercury switch. If you rock a mercury switch back and forth, it will make the light flicker. Unfortunately, in order to operate the flicker from a switch on the ground, I would have to run another wire from the sign to the switch on the ground. I ran out of time and after I used all the wire I had, I still was not able to get the switch out of the shot, so, they put me in an old trench coat and let me sit on the ground in front of the hotel like a homeless person while I wiggled my mercury switch during the shot. They used several cameras on this shot but they ended up not using the camera angle that I was in. I ended up on the cutting room floor, but my flickering sign is in the movie. John was thrilled, and he presented me with my badge of honor, one of his terrycloth caps. I was the only

The Cheap Detective – The Cast

electrician at that time, other than Jim Plannette, to ever receive a John Alonzo terrycloth cap, and I still have it.

Ann-Margaret's Good Wishes

HOOPER (1978)

Starring:	Burt Reynolds, Jan-Michael Vincent, Sally Field, Brian Keith
Director:	Hal Needham
Cinematographer:	Bobby Byrne
Lighting Gaffer:	James Boyle
Studio Best Boy:	Paul Caven

I was the Studio Best Boy on this movie. Some shows divide the best boy responsibilities between a company best boy and a studio best boy. Most of my career I was the company best boy, but this time I was hired as the studio best boy. I did not go with them on location to Alabama. They shot there first, filming the end sequence. I worked with them from February through March of 1978 when they came back to Los Angeles. The cameraman, Bobby Byrne, was an old friend of mine. He used to be the camera operator for Laszlo Kovacs. Hal Needham was the Director. Hal had been Burt's stunt double for years and I had worked with him several times including on *Nickelodeon.* This was his second directorial outing, the first being *Smokey and the Bandit.* He understandably was known for his stunt movies and this was no exception.

The route the car took for the huge climactic stunt sequence, where they blow up half the town, blow up a bridge, then jump the car over the river, was referred to by the crew as "Damnation Alley." It was staged at the abandoned Northington General Hospital, a World War II military hospital in Tuscaloosa, Alabama, which had also been used as married-student housing by The University of Alabama. After they filmed the annihilation of most of the hospital buildings (including a large smokestack) in Damnation Alley, the lot was cleared and the University Mall complex was built on the site.

The name Hooper is a reference to the name "Hooker" as in Buddy Joe Hooker (a famous stuntman who worked on the show). Buddy Joe Hooker's name even appears on a strip of tape on a drawer in "Sonny

Hooper's" trailer. It can be seen over Burt's shoulder, early in the movie, in the scene where Sonny (Burt) and Cully (James Best) do their Roy Rogers' sidekick and James Stewart impressions. Jim Best was a great guy. I worked with him before on another show with Burt, *Nickelodeon.*

This was my fourth and last picture with Burt. Burt is one of my all-time favorite actors. He was a great guy. His most endearing characteristic was that he never took himself seriously. He laughed about his stardom. He is one of those who hung out with the crew and knew everyone's name. This was my second picture with Jan-Michael Vincent, the first being *Baby Blue Marine.* It was also my second show with Sally Field. I worked with her on the TV drama, *Sybil.* Also, my second picture with Brian Keith, the first being *Nickelodeon.* Robert Klein plays the film director in the movie. His last lines in the show, about film being "little pieces of time", is a paraphrased quote of the monolog by Brian Keith's character at the end of *Nickelodeon* which I mentioned before and also the title of a book by Peter Bogdanovich. In fact, it is said that Robert Klein's character was based on Peter Bogdanovich. If so, I am not sure the characterization of Peter in this film was totally fair. Peter can be very demanding and impertinent to producers, but he was never diabolical like this character portrays him.

EVERY WHICH WAY BUT LOOSE (1978)

Starring: Clint Eastwood, Sondra Locke, Geoffrey Lewis, Beverly D'Angelo, Ruth Gordon

Director: James Fargo

Cinematographer: Rex Metz

Lighting Gaffer: Don Nygren

Best Boy: Paul Caven (screen credit)

When I first read this script, I remember thinking to myself, "You have got to be kidding, Clint Eastwood is doing a road movie with a monkey; he starts following a girl singer around the country, and the climax of the film is when he finds out that the girl is pimping for her gay boyfriend? Seriously?" I thought, "This is going to be a loser!" I justified my participation by saying to myself, "I don't write 'em I just light 'em." Well, it shows you how wrong I can be. *Every Which Way But Loose* was Clint Eastwood's highest grossing film and remained so until *Unforgiven* in 1992.

The film had a good cast. Ruth Gordon, of course, was a pro. Bill McKinney, from *Deliverance,* played one of the motorcycle gang. Sondra Locke did several of Clint Eastwood's movies. In my personal opinion she was basically a no-talent. Of course, we all know what my opinion is worth. Geoffrey Lewis and Beverly DiAngelo, I think, did a super job.

I think one thing that added to the popularity of the show was the country music. There were several country music super stars in this show who did not even receive screen credit: Charlie Rich, Mel Tillis, and Phil Everly. I am not sure why they did not receive screen credit, but they did not… and I did! Go figure!

We filmed in a couple of classic country music locations. The Palomino Club in the San Fernando Valley was host to all the top country performers in its day. I don't think it's even there anymore. We also filmed in Nudies, the renowned clothing store owned by the legendary Nudie Cohn. Nudie suits were the uniform of the day for all the classic country stars, from Hank Williams to Marty Stuart. They were known for their wild patterns in glitter and sequins. When country stars switched to Levis and t-shirts, Nudies went by the wayside.

As I mentioned, this was a road picture. We filmed in the spring of 1978 in Southern California, Albuquerque, Taos and Santa Fe, New Mexico, as well as locations around Denver, Colorado. I never unpacked my suitcase.

Clyde, the orangutan, was of course, the real star of the show. In reality, they had three Clydes. The trainers had a Clyde for every trick. Like most trained animals on the set, we knew not to pay any attention to them because they need to concentrate on what the trainers want them to do. You basically have to ignore them. The orangutans, however, seemed to want the attention. When the trainers would walk them to the set, they would reach out for you. What they wanted to do was pinch the skin in back of your elbow. It was very strange!

The orangutans, however, did not always respond to the trainer's commands. When it came time to shoot the scene where Clyde flips the finger from the back of the camper, the orangutan trained to do that, would not do it. The trainer said he would go in the camper and get the orangutan to do what he was trained to do. As we all stood there waiting for him to get the orangutan back in line so we could shoot, suddenly there came a hell of a ruckus from inside the camper. The camper started to rock violently back and forth. The door flew open, and Clyde threw the trainer out on his ear and flipped him the finger. They are very strong animals; they are classified as great apes. The trainer got up, shook himself off and bravely charged back into the camper. I do not know what went on inside that camper the second time, but the trainer emerged and said expressionlessly, "Let's shoot it." We did, and Clyde flipped the finger right on cue.

Every Which Way But Loose – The Cast and Crew in Action

Clint Eastwood – The Fight

Clint Eastwood – The Fight

Clint Eastwood Fishing

Clyde & The Finger

THE RUNNER STUMBLES (1978)

Starring:	Dick Van Dyke, Kathleen Quinlan, Maureen Stapleton, Ray Bolger, Tammy Grimes, Beau Bridges
Director:	Stanley Kramer
Cinematographer:	Laszlo Kovacs
Lighting Gaffer:	Aggie Aguilar
Best Boy:	Paul Caven

I really liked this movie; although it never did well commercially. I think that was because some people just could not see Dick Van Dyke in a dramatic role. He was more generally known as a comedic actor. This was definitely a dark drama, and I think he did a marvelous job. It was based on a play by the same name, which was based on a true story about a Catholic priest who had been banished to an economically depressed old mining town and sees it as a dead end. He asks the Archbishop for a nun to replace the two old and sickly nuns in the parish convent. The Archbishop sends him a young, energetic nun whose enthusiasm not only motivates her students to do better, but also revives his spirit that had been lost long ago. They fall in love and both struggle with the violation of their vows. When she turns up dead, he is accused of her murder. Although he is found to be innocent of the murder, he must live the rest of his life with the reality that he has lost everything he loved, not only the priesthood, but the woman he loved.

This movie was directed by the legendary director Stanley Kramer, who directed such classics as: *Guess Who's Coming to Dinner, Judgment at Nuremberg,* and *Inherit the Wind.* This would be the last film he would direct. I considered it an honor to have worked with such a renowned director and a very warm-hearted person.

The cast was equally as well-known and all very friendly: Dick Van Dyke, Kathleen Quinlan, Maureen Stapleton, Tammy Grimes, Beau Bridges, and the great Ray Bolger. This was my second show with Ray Bolger, and his last film. He was such a professional and a charming person.

We filmed the movie in the summer of 1978 in Roslyn, Washington. It was definitely an economically depressed old mining town. Roslyn would later be the location for the 1990's TV shows *Northern Exposure* and *Twin Peaks*.

The Runner Stumbles – The Cast

Dick Van Dyke

Dick Van Dyke & Kathleen Quinlan

Billy Jayne

Kathleen Quinlan, Maureen Stapleton,
Dick Van Dyke, Tammy Grimes

The Runner Stumbles – The Cast and Crew In Action

Dick Van Dyke & Kathleen Quinlan – The Sack Race

Kathleen Quinlan – The Sack Race

Paul Caven, Aggie Aguilar, Chris Strong Ben McNulty & Leroy Hershkowitz

Dick Van Dyke, Katheen Quinlan & Crew

The Crew
(Photo by Elliott Marks Company Still Photographer)

109

HEART BEAT (1978)

Starring:	Nick Nolte, Sissy Spacek, John Heard, Ann Dusenberry, Ray Sharkey
Director:	John Byrum
Cinematographer:	Laszlo Kovacs
Lighting Gaffer:	Aggie Aguilar
Best Boy:	Paul Caven (screen credit)

This was a film biography of Jack Kerouac (played by John Heard) during the writing of his classic book, *On The Road,* which chronicled the life of his best friend Neal Cassady (played by Nick Nolte) and the woman who loved them both, Carolyn Cassady (played by Sissy Spacek). The book *On the Road* was said to spawn the "Beatnik Era" in the 1950s. The movie chronicles an open love triangle during a time when such things were unheard of. My favorite line in the film was at the end when Jack asks Carolyn, "What did we do wrong?" She replies, "We didn't do anything wrong, we just did it first."

John Byrum wrote and directed this film. He was also one of the writers of *Harry and Walter Go to New York* which we worked on, so when he was looking for a cinematographer for his film, he called Laszlo. The character in the film, Ira, played by Ray Sharkey, was based on the contemporary shock poet Allen Ginsberg, who was a friend of Jack Kerouac. Jack Kerouac's only daughter, Jan Kerouac, worked as an extra on the film. The real Carolyn Cassady (the only one of the trio still alive at the time) visited the set and said the script accurately portrayed the life she lived; the love, the pain, and the role the three of them played in the advent of the free love generation of the 1960s.

We filmed this movie in Los Angeles and San Francisco in the fall of 1978. The exterior scenes of their house in the suburbs were filmed in an area of Downey, California, that was vacated and scheduled for demolition to make way for a new freeway. In a couple of scenes we see that the landscaping in front of their house was marijuana plants. They used real marijuana plants in pots that the prop man came up with…no names! On this show, as well as most shows, they hire local off-duty or retired police to handle traffic control. The funny part was that when it came time to film the scenes with the marijuana plants, the word went out to the production assistants to have the cops go to lunch. As soon as we finished filming those scenes, the prop man scooped up the potted pot plants and disappeared. The cops never knew.

Toward the end of the film there is a scene in a beatnik bar set called "Fat's Station." There's a close-up of two beatniks who are snapping their fingers which was the way beatniks applauded. Those two beatniks were Laszlo and his best friend Vilmos Zsigmond.

Heart Beat – The Cast

Nick Nolte

Nick Nolte, Sunshine Parker & Girl Extra

Heart Beat – The Cast & Crew In Action

Chris Strong & Paul Caven

John Byrum

Heart Beat – The Cast & Crew In Action (con't)

Bus Dolly & Nick Nolte Driving Bus

Bus Dolly with John Byrum

Bus Dolly on The Road

PAUL CAVEN

THE ELECTRIC HORSEMAN (1978)

Starring: Robert Redford, Jane Fonda, Willie Nelson, Valerie Perrine, John Saxon and Wilford Brimley

Director: Sidney Pollack

Cinematographer: Owen Roizman

Lighting Gaffer: Joe Pender/Ted Holt

My old buddy Joe Pender was the gaffer at the beginning of this show. Joe had worked with Aggie and me on a few other films, including *Shampoo,* and I had worked for him before. So, when Joe got this job, he called me. Unfortunately, Joe was a fairly new gaffer, and some felt this movie was too big of a job for him. I don't think they gave him a chance. He was eventually let go. I knew the new gaffer, Teddy Holt, but had never worked with him before. I was kept on the show for a while after Joe left, but eventually Teddy wanted his own crew on the show. That is the way it works in this business, so I did not work on the whole film. I worked on all of the Las Vegas scenes and some of the scenes in St. George, Utah. They also filmed in Grafton and Zion National Park in Utah.

I worked on the film from October to December of 1978. We spent six weeks in Las Vegas; that was a real education. We filmed all the casino scenes in Caesar's Palace late at night. Some of the stuff you see in casinos late at night is a real eye opener; the winners and the losers. One night, I saw a guy playing black jack who had apparently lost everything. He suddenly ripped the shirt off his back and threw it down on the table and said, "Here, you might as well take this too!" and stormed out. The dealer just picked the shirt up, threw it under the table and dealt the next hand. The casino people told us it happens all the time.

This was my first of two pictures with Robert Redford and the first of two pictures with Jane Fonda. They were both very, very nice.

The director, Sydney Pollack, gave himself a small part in the movie. You can see him in a scene where Jane is walking through the casino. He, with lipstick all over his face, stops her and says, "Hallie, Hallie Martin we met in New York." She says, while still walking, "Did we like each other?" and keeps on walking.

This was Willie Nelson's first movie. He is a fantastic guy. He just wanted to hang out with the crew. On the first scene we filmed with him, they rehearsed it and then, as usual, they released the actors to go to make up and wardrobe while we use stand-ins to line up the camera and light the scene. The other actor in the scene (Valerie Perrine) left, but Willie just sat there talking with the guys. The assistant director said, "Willie you can go now." Willie said, "No that's ok, I'll just sit a spell." The assistant director said, "Ah, no, you see, we hire stand-ins to sit here, and you need to go to make up." Willie looked at him and said, "Really?" the assistant director just nodded, and Willie reluctantly got up and went to makeup.

Willie did not have any members of his band with him on this movie, but he did bring his famous guitar with the hole in it. Some nights after work, he would sneak out and go to some of the little cowboy bars downtown and asked the house band if he could sit in. When we found out about this we asked him to let us know next time he was going to play. One day on the set he told us where he was going to go that night. It was a tiny little hole-in-the-wall bar way out of town. Willie told them we were coming so they set up a couple of rows of chairs in front of the bandstand. It was the middle of the week so the place was almost empty when we showed up. There were just a few people at a couple of tables in the back of the room. We sat down while Willie warmed up. As soon as he started to play it dawned on the people in the back who it was. They started to wander up closer when they suddenly realized that it was not only Willie Nelson but Robert Redford and Jane Fonda who were sitting right there. They rushed back to the back of the room to the pay phones and started calling all their friends. Willie played for over an hour. He played all his big hits. By the end, the place was nearly packed. Willie thanked everybody and then thanked the band. He put his guitar back in its case and we all walked out. What a night!

Denise was with me in Las Vegas during Thanksgiving. Caesar's Palace was offering a Thanksgiving dinner. Several of us decided to go. We all sat at one big banquet table. It turned out to be much more than a Thanksgiving dinner. It was a seven-course feast;

everything from soup to nuts including a different bottle of wine with each course. I have never eaten so much food or drunk so much wine in my life. I suddenly started to worry about how much this Thanksgiving spread was going to cost. There was no menu. It was all a package. When we were all finished we sat there waiting for the bad news. We all breathed a collective sigh of relief when they told us that Caesar's Palace was "comping" our meal. Hail Caesar!

The "Electric Suit" Redford wears was set up by the special effects crew. The lights were battery operated with the batteries being in the saddle bags. It was kind of a delicate rig, he had to be careful not to rock too much in the saddle. One time he rocked too far back in the saddle and he broke a couple of the bulbs and they burnt a hole in the back of his pants. After that they would wait to plug it in until just before the shot.

The horse on the show was a beautiful 5-year-old bay named "Let's Merge." After the show, Redford bought the horse and kept it for 18 years until it passed away. It was a magnificent animal.

On a side note, this was another show that I worked on with my old stuntman friend, Ralph Garrett.

The Electric Horseman – The Cast

Robert Redford "Electric"

Robert Redford "Un-electric"

Robert Redford & Jane Fonda

Robert Redford & Jane Fonda

The Horse Wrangler & Robert Redford

117

THE BALTIMORE BULLET (1978)

Starring:	James Coburn, Omar Sharif, Bruce Boxleitner and Ronnee Blakely
Director:	Robert Ellis Miller
Cinematographer:	Jim Crabe
Lighting Gaffer:	Aggie Aguilar
Best Boy:	Paul Caven

We filmed this movie March through May of 1979 in the Los Angeles area and in New Orleans, Louisiana. It was a pleasure to work with James Coburn and Omar Sharif; they were both very cordial. Bruce Boxleitner was essentially a TV actor best known for his TV show *Scarecrow and Mrs. King.* Ronnee Blakely was best known for her supporting role in the movie *Nashville,* but basically, she was a musician and composer. The show was pretty mediocre. It did not do well at the box office. It was mostly about pool hustling and had a lot of stars from the pool playing world, 'Machine Gun' Lou Butera, Steve Mizerak, and Irving Crane. This was our second show with Jimmy Crabe. He was a wonderful person and a great cameraman.

We filmed most of the scenes with Omar Sharif in New Orleans—the card game, the exterior of the hotel and the funeral procession. One day Omar sent his cousin, who closely resembles Omar, to the set to pick up some script changes. The assistant director, mistaking him for Omar, sent him to makeup and wardrobe to get ready for the next scene. It was then that they discovered it was not Omar.

New Orleans' cuisine is wonderfully diverse. They have French restaurants, Creole restaurants, Cajun restaurants just about any kind of food you want and it's all delicious.

The Baltimore Bullet – The Cast

Omar Sharif

James Coburn's Best Wishes

The Baltimore Bullet – Shooting On Location

Shooting in New Orleans

New Orleans Street Musician

New Orleans Funeral Marching Band

119

BEFORE AND AFTER (1979)

Starring:	Patty Duke, Bradford Dillman, Barbara Feldon, Conchata Ferrell, Kenneth Mars, Betty White
Director:	Kim Friedman
Cinematographer:	Brianne Murphy
Lighting Gaffer:	Aggie Aguilar
Best Boy:	Paul Caven

This was a TV movie of the week that we filmed in Seattle in June of 1979. It is a story about an overweight housewife (Patty Duke) who has to confront her weight problem when her husband (Bradford Dillman) leaves her because of it. She has a happily married overweight friend (Conchata Ferrell) and an unhappy thin, engaged friend (Barbara Feldon), who is starving herself to fit into her grandmother's wedding gown. Patty Duke's character diets and exercises to reach her goal weight in time for the wedding; but her thin friend collapses at the reception due to her rigorous dieting. The story has a lot to say about the psychological effects on women whose self-esteem is centered on the pressures of society's obsession with being thin. Being healthy and happy is more important.

It had a marvelous cast. Patty was very friendly. We had worked with Kenneth Mars years before on *What's Up Doc?* Betty White was a hoot. She just enjoys every minute of life; God bless her! Conchata Ferrell, years later, landed the role as Bertha on *Two and a Half Men.*

This was a "Chick-Flick" (in the vernacular of the day) in more ways than one. Besides the story line and all the women in the cast, it had a female director (Kim Friedman), who was very talented and a female cinematographer (Brianne Murphy), who was equally as talented. Brianne, a year after this film, became the first female member of the American Society of Cinematographers. She won a Daytime Emmy, was nominated for three Primetime Emmy's, and won the Women in Film Crystal Award in 1984. She led a very colorful life. She was a trick rider for a rodeo one season. She was a clown for the Ringling Brothers Circus. She worked her way up from a photographer to a low budget cinematographer to a major Hollywood cinematographer. She was quite a woman. My only regret is that this was our only picture with Bri.

One day we were scheduled to shoot in a house in Seattle. We had scouted the location days before and had a plan. On the day we were to shoot the location, we arrived early in the morning and unloaded our lights and cables from our truck. We watched a rehearsal and after the rehearsal, we started lighting the set. On her way back to her motor home after the rehearsal, the director saw another house she liked better. We were half way finished lighting the scene when the word came down that they decided to film in the other house instead. We had to wrap everything back to our trucks, move down the street and start the process all over again. That was a long day!

Maybe I should explain what effort and preparation goes on before the director can say "Action". First, we get a script and usually a shooting schedule. Prior to filming, the location manager takes the director, assistant director, the art director, the cinematographer, the lighting gaffer, the lighting best boy, the key grip and his best boy, and any other department head that may need to be involved, to scout all the locations they picked to film.

When we scout each location I need to know what the basic camera angles are going to be, so I know where I can park our generator and be out of the shot. From the generator, I need to know how many feet of cable I am going to need to reach the set. I need to know if there is anything special I may need to order. When we arrive to shoot the location that we have scouted, we can get started right away running our cables and getting our lights all set up while they rehearse the scene. Then we get to work.

Changing the location in mid-stream means we not only have to completely wrap the old location, cable, lights, everything and load our truck to move down the street, but also I need to go scout the new location to see what we need there. Then we unload the trucks and start all over again. The director, Kim Friedman, was very nice but she had only been directing for three years at the time. A more experienced director might have seen that other house when they were out scouting with the location manager days ahead of the rest of us. This change cost the production company a lot of time and money.

Before and After – The Cast and Crew

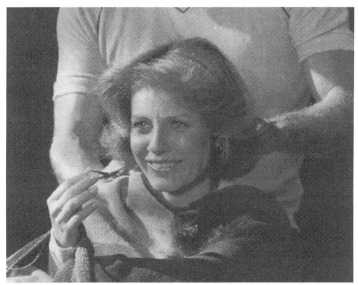

Patty Duke

Brianne Murphy & Patty Duke

HOW TO BEAT THE HIGH CO$T OF LIVING (1979)

Starring: Susan Saint James, Jane Curtin, Jessica Lange, Richard Benjamin, Eddie Albert, Dabney Coleman and Fred Willard

Director: Robert Scheerer

Cinematographer: Jim Crabe

Lighting Gaffer: Aggie Aguilar

Best Boy: Paul Caven (screen credit)

It is Oregon, present time. Three friends, Jane, Elaine and Louise are all feeling the effects of inflation and cannot afford, as the title states, the high cost of living. The local mall is having a contest that features a giant money ball where one lucky contestant will have one minute to grab all the money they can as it swirls all around them. Elaine comes up with a plan to steal the money from the money ball and split it between the three of them. So, of course, one catastrophe after another interferes with them achieving their goal.

This was a cute little comedy with a good cast. It was my first of three pictures with Jessica Lange. Susan Saint James was really friendly with the crew. She knew most everyone's name. This was Jane Curtin's first movie. I have mentioned before that sometimes, stand-up comedians do not make good actors. I also noted that most of the former SNL comedians I've worked with (Gilda Radner excepted) were not very friendly and Jane Curtin was no exception. Her old SNL co-star Garrett Morris also had a bit part in this show. Working with these three female co-stars was fascinating. Whenever all three were in the same shot, it was always a contest to see which one would be the last one on the set. You could see them looking out the window of their motor homes to see if the others were on their way yet.

Richard Benjamin was also very friendly with the crew. Eddie Albert was another old pro. He had been in the business a long time. Our stunt friends Ralph and Donna Garrett both worked on this film. Ralph even had a small speaking part. Donna was the stunt double for

Jane Curtin and did the stunt where the light pole, with Jane perched on it, falls into the money ball.

We filmed it in September and October of 1979 in Oregon. The storyline required a mall that is next to a river and they found one in Eugene, Oregon. We filmed most of the mall scenes late at night when the mall was closed. When we were shooting the river scenes, we were so spread out that we had a hard time communicating with our crew and our generator operator. This was before the days when everyone on the set was issued walkie-talkies. Because we were in Eugene, Oregon, the home of the University of Oregon Ducks, I had no problem finding duck calls. I set up a series of different calls for different people on our crew. Our improvised communication system worked pretty well.

This was my third and final picture with Jimmy Crabe. As I stated before, he was a wonderful person. Unfortunately, he died at the age of 57, a great loss. He was a very talented cinematographer. He was nominated for an Academy Award for the movie *The Formula*. He was nominated for two ASC awards. He won two Primetime Emmy Awards and was nominated for three other Primetime Emmys including the first show I worked with him on, *The Entertainer*. He did such classic films as *The China Syndrome, Rocky,* and *Night Shift*. I miss Jimmy Crabe.

How to Beat the High Cost of Living – The Cast

**Jessica Lange &
Susan Saint James**

**Susan Saint James &
Jane Curtain**

Susan Saint James' Good Wishes

THE INFLUENCE OF INDEPENDENTS

The mid 1960s, the 1970s and the early 1980s were the apex of the Second Golden Age of movies. As the old studio system of the 1930s and 1940s completely broke down, a new generation of filmmakers came to prominence. They influenced the types of films being made, their production and marketing, and the way major studios approached film-making. Now the director, rather than the studio, had complete control. From this new cinematic freedom came such movies as: *Bonnie and Clyde, The Graduate, Easy Rider, King of Marvin Gardens, Deliverance, Paper Moon and Shampoo.*

All this freedom spawned innovations in lighting as well. We changed from DC power to AC power. They developed new lights with new technologies. It would create decades of change—change that is still going on today.

THE DECLARATION OF INDEPENDENTS

THE POSTMAN ALWAYS RINGS TWICE (1980)

Starring:	Jack Nicholson, Jessica Lange, John Colicos
Director:	Robert Rafelson
Cinematographer:	Sven Nykvist
Lighting Gaffer:	Aggie Aguilar
Best Boy:	Paul Caven

This was a steamy remake of the 1940s classic film of the same name with Lana Turner, John Garfield, and Cecil Kellaway. This was my second picture with Jack Nicholson, the first being *The King of Marvin Gardens* also directed by Bob Rafelson. It was also my second picture in a row with Jessica Lange.

We filmed this movie between February and April of 1980. Some of it was filmed in and around the Los Angeles area, but the majority of it was filmed on a private ranch in the Santa Inez Mountains north of Santa Barbara, California. The "Twin Oaks" restaurant set where most of the filming takes place was built there. The art director, Oscar winning George Jenkins, and the construction department built the entire restaurant set and garage from scratch and then took it all down at the end of shooting.

We stayed in Santa Barbara during the week while we were

shooting there but we were able to go home on the weekends. Santa Barbara is about a two-hour drive from Los Angeles. During the Los Angeles Lakers play-off run that year, Denise and I had tickets for a home play-off game at the Los Angeles Forum, but I was not going to be able to go because I could not get there and back in time. I was talking to Jack Nicholson during the day and asked if he was going to the game. He was going, of course, so I told him that I had tickets but I was not going to be able to go. He said, "Well you can hitch a ride with me, Paulie." (He always called me Paulie.) So, after work that night, Jack, Bob Rafelson, and I got into Bob's rental car and drove to the Santa Barbara airport, hopped into a Lear Jet and took the ten-minute flight to LAX, then we jumped into a waiting limo and drove to the Los Angeles Forum.

Jack and Bob went to Jack's courtside seats, and I joined Denise up in our seats. After the game, it took me a little more time than Jack and Bob to get out to the limo. What was really cool was there was a crowd of people and paparazzi around the limo, some of them taking pictures when I walked up. I went through the crowd and jumped in the limo as people flashed pictures wondering who I was. We went back to LAX, boarded the Lear Jet, and flew back to Santa Barbara. What a night!

Sven Nykvist was considered by many in the industry to be one of the world's greatest cinematographers. He worked for many years with the legendary Swedish director Ingmar Bergman. During his long career that spanned almost half a century, he perfected the art of cinematography to its most simple attribute. He helped give the films he worked on the simplest and most natural look imaginable, so that the emotion of the scene could be played out on the faces without the light becoming intrusive. With him, it was all about lighting. Aggie likes to light the whole set, if it is in the shot, it gets a light on it. Sometimes, as Aggie was finishing lighting a set, Sven would joke in his Swedish accent, "Aggie, too many lights" then he and Aggie would laugh but Sven never turned any of Aggies light off. This was the first of four movies that Aggie and I worked on with Sven. He was a brilliant man, a quiet genius who was unassuming with a good sense of humor. He was a delightful person.

There were some great actors in this show: Anjelica Houston (who was Jack's on and off girlfriend), Michael Lerner who I had worked with before on *The Baltimore Bullet*, John Ryan who I worked with on *The King of Marvin Gardens*, and Christopher Lloyd had a small bit part at the opening of the show.

129

The Postman Always Rings Twice – The Cast

Jessica Lange & Jack Nicholson

Jessica Lange

**Jack Nicholson's
Good Wishes**
(Photo by Carol McCullough)

**Jessica Lange's
Good Wishes**
(Photo by Carol McCullough)

The Postman Always Rings Twice – The Crew

Sven Nykvist

The Lighting Crew: Paul Caven, Jon O'Neil, Sven Nykvist,
Tom Baronni, Aggie, Ray Banagan, & our truck driver

MOVIOLA: THE SCARLETT O'HARA WAR (1980)

Starring: Tony Curtis, Harold Gould, Carrie Nye, Sharon Gless, Bill Macy

Director: John Erman

Cinematographer: Gayne Rescher

Lighting Gaffer: Thor Sundby

Based on part of a 1979 Hollywood novel by Garson Kanin, "The Scarlett O'Hara Wars" covers producer David O. Selznick's lengthy search for the right actress to play Margaret Mitchell's Scarlett O'Hara in his 1939 production of "Gone with the Wind." This television film was one of three episodes adapted from the Kanin novel for a limited television series, the others being "The Silent Lovers" and "This Year's Blonde."

It had a good cast. It was nominated for a Golden Globe Award for Best TV Series and it won Primetime Emmy Awards for Make-up and Costume Design. It was nominated for Primetime Emmy Awards for Best Director-John Erman, Best Leading Actor - Tony Curtis who plays David O. Selznick, Best Supporting Actor - Harold Gould who plays Louis B. Mayer, and Best Supporting Actress - Carrie Nye who plays Tallulah Bankhead. We filmed it in and around the Los Angeles area and at the Warner Brothers Studio in April and May of 1980.

Moviola: The Scarlett O'Hara War: The Cast

Tony Curtis
(Photo Credit: Public Domain)

ON GOLDEN POND (1980)

Starring:	Katharine Hepburn, Henry Fonda, Jane Fonda, Doug McKeon, Dabney Coleman and William Lanteau
Director:	Mark Rydell
Cinematographer:	Billy Williams
Lighting Gaffer:	Aggie Aguilar
Best Boy:	Paul Caven (screen credit)

There were many films over my 40-year career that I enjoyed working on, but when people ask me which film I am the most proud of, it is by far *On Golden Pond*. It was the thrill of a lifetime to be able to work with Katharine Hepburn and Henry Fonda. Like I have said many times, the old pros were the best to work with.

This film won 37 American and international awards. It won three Academy Awards. Henry Fonda, Katharine Hepburn, and Ernest Thompson all won Oscars. Jane Fonda, Mark Rydel, and Billy Williams were all nominated for Academy Awards.

We filmed from July through September of 1980. At that time there was an actors' strike in Hollywood. The Screen Actors Guild allowed an exemption for this film realizing that Henry only had so much time left, and if the film did not get done that summer, it would be delayed another year. This was indeed Henry's last movie. He did one other TV movie later that year, but he passed away in 1982.

Norman Thayer, played by Henry Fonda, a retired professor and his wife Ethel, played by Katharine Hepburn, had a summer cottage on Golden Pond their entire married life. This summer their daughter Chelsea, played by Jane Fonda, whom they have not seen for years, feels the need to be there for Norman's birthday. She and her fiancé, played by Dabney Coleman, are on their way to Europe the next day so she asks her parents if they would take care of her fiancé's son for a couple of weeks until they get back. When they return, they are married, and after her time away, Chelsea realizes that her stepson has the relationship with her father that she always wanted.

133

On the first day of filming, Katharine asked Henry if he would please wear a particular brown Fedora in the opening scene, so he did. It turned out that the hat belonged to Spencer Tracy. Henry, overwhelmed with the gesture, painted a still life watercolor of the three hats he wore in the film, including the brown Fedora. He titled the painting "Norman Thayer," his character's name, and gave the original to Katharine Hepburn as a gift. He had 200 lithographs made of the painting and sent one to every person who worked on the film. Each copy was numbered and personally signed by Hank, thanking each member of the crew by name. On my painting he wrote, "For Paul warmest fond wishes, Hank." In her autobiography, Katharine wrote that she later gave the original painting to screenwriter Ernest Thompson because after Fonda's death, she found the painting to be a sad reminder of Henry and Spencer Tracy. For me, it is my greatest treasure, a caring memento from Hank that hangs above my mantle.

It was no secret that Henry's relationship with Jane had been strained over the years, very similar to the relationship between Norman and Chelsea in this film. The scene between Chelsea and Norman where she tells him she wants to be his friend mirrored the real-life relationship between father and daughter. During one take in that intimate scene between the two of them, Jane unexpectedly, but lovingly, put her hand on her father's arm. Henry started to cry and ducked his head away from the camera, embarrassed by his tears. That take appears in the final film. I believe Henry and Jane reconciled at that very loving on-screen moment. Jane had bought the rights to the film years before, I believe, with the intention of doing just that in the only way these two actors could. They could not do it in real life as father and daughter, but they could do it as two characters playing a father and daughter.

There were two young boys on the boat dock gas station that Henry has a confrontation with. The one he speaks to was Christopher Rydell, Mark Rydell's son. The other boy was Troy Garity, Jane's son and Henry's grandson.

We stayed at a resort at Lake Winnipesauke, New Hampshire. The Golden Pond was actually Squam Lake, New Hampshire. The majority of the film was shot in a remote cabin on the lake down a narrow dirt road. Our 40 foot trucks were all parked about a mile away back at a clearing on the road. This meant we needed to completely unload our truck and haul everything up to the set. But, after we got the cabin rigged with lights hanging in the ceiling and elsewhere, it was not as difficult to light each individual shot.

One of the things I loved about filming on the lake was watching and listening to the loons. They are large, beautiful, black and white birds with a wonderfully haunting call. You can hear their eerie cries echoing across the water. You can watch them effortlessly dive deep into the water to catch fish. They are fascinating birds.

On Golden Pond – The Cast

**Henry Fonda and
Katherine Hepburn**
(Photo by Aggie Aguilar)

Jane Fonda's Good Wishes

Norman Thayer – Hats (Lithograph of Original Painting by Henry Fonda)

WRONG IS RIGHT (1981)

Starring:	Sean Connery, George Grizzard, Robert Conrad, Katharine Ross, John Saxon, Henry Silva, Leslie Nielsen, Robert Webber, Rosalind Cash, Dean Stockwell
Director:	Richard Brooks
Cinematographer:	Fred Koenekamp
Lighting Gaffer:	Gene Stout

This was a black comedy that, in retrospect, was prophetic. Although we filmed this from March through May of 1981, the story line is about Mideast Arab terrorists who threaten to blow up New York with a stolen atomic bomb. In fact, it shows the two suitcases containing the bombs perched on top of the World Trade Center.

The movie did not do very well at the box office despite an all-star cast, possibly because the director, Richard Brooks, who also wrote the screenplay, was primarily a writer not a director. He had a tendency to be obsessive. He guarded the script. It was only doled out a little at a time. No one ever got a complete script during the filming.

Sean Connery was fantastic, of course, he's Scottish. It was a real kick to work with James Bond. Although this was not a James Bond movie, he will always be, "Bond, James Bond." I had worked with John Saxon before on *The Electric Horseman.* My favorite actor on this show was Leslie Nielsen. I had worked with him a few times on TV shows years before. He was a great practical joker. His favorite thing was a little fart machine that he had for years. It was a small section of a rubber bicycle tube, sealed at both ends with a tiny hole in one end that he would hold in his hand. When he put the hole against his palm and squeezed the tube, it sounded just like a fart. He loved it. He would stand in a group or in an elevator and squeeze one off and wait for the reaction. It worked every time. They don't make 'em like Leslie anymore.

I did not work on the whole film; I only worked on the studio scenes. But, after the show was over, I was the gaffer for the special effect's miniatures shooting. They had several miniatures of New York landmarks that we were going to demolish. One day we had a miniature of the Empire State Building that we were going to blow up in slow motion. The camera, at normal speed, exposes 24 frames of film per second. To film in slow motion, you need to speed the camera up to expose hundreds of frames per second, depending on how slow you want it to look. When it gets played at the theater at normal speed it appears to be in slow motion. The problem with filming at high speeds for us is the fact that the more frames per second, the more light you need to expose the film at the proper exposure. I had 20 arc lights in the catwalk circling the set. We spent most of the day setting up the shot. When we were ready to shoot, I told my crew to make sure their arcs had fresh carbons in them then, for safety reasons, I cleared all my guys off of the catwalks above the set and they rolled the high-speed cameras. They cued the special effects man to detonate the explosives. Unfortunately, one of my guys had left his empty styrofoam coffee cup sitting on the catwalks above the set. The compression of the explosion knocked the cup off the catwalk and right down into the middle of the shot. When they looked at the replay on video, what they saw was a King Kong size styrofoam coffee cup floating in slow motion past the exploding Empire State building. Luckily it was set up so that the explosion did not actually destroy the miniature, and we were able to reshoot. But, thereafter, all styrofoam cups were banned from the set!

GOLIATH AWAITS (1981)

Starring:	Mark Harmon, Christopher Lee, Eddie Albert, John Carradine, Alex Cord, Robert Forster, Frank Gorshin and Emma Samms
Director:	Kevin Connor
Cinematographer:	Al Francis
Lighting Gaffer:	Jim Lott

This was a TV movie of the week. We filmed at Warner Brothers Studio and at the RMS Queen Mary in Long Beach, California, in June and July of 1981. The story line was that during World War II, the passenger liner "Goliath" is sunk by a German submarine. Portions of the ship's hull remain airtight at the bottom of the ocean, and some of the passengers and crew survive. Over the decades, they build a rigidly regulated society completely isolated from the surface world, until in contemporary times a diving team begins to explore the wreck.

It had an all-star cast but did not do well in the TV ratings. I think that the story line was a little too far-fetched. The actors were all fine. I had worked with Eddie Albert just a couple of years before on *How to Beat the High Cost of Living.*

I got hired because I had worked with the gaffer Jim Lott many times before, including both of us working together as lighting techs on *Casey's Shadow.* I had also worked with the cameraman Al Francis on the first episode of the TV series *The Streets of San Francisco.*

FRANCES (1981)

Starring:	Jessica Lange, Kim Stanley, Sam Shepard, Bart Burns
Director:	Graeme Clifford
Cinematographer:	Laszlo Kovacs
Lighting Gaffer:	Aggie Aguilar
Best Boy:	Paul Caven (screen credit)

We shot this film from December 1981 through February 1982 in and around Los Angeles and Seattle, Washington. This was a dark drama about the tragic life of actress Frances Farmer. It is, however, essentially a love story between Frances (played by Jessica Lange) and Harry York (played by Sam Shepard), who loves her for who she is in spite of herself.

Harry comes in and out of Frances' life as a stabilizing factor. She was a strong-willed woman in a time when that was not acceptable behavior for a contract studio actress. She rebelled against the studio system and became an outcast. Her mother (played by Kim Stanley), who wanted Frances to be a famous movie star so she could be famous too, had her committed. While a mental patient, she was given a lobotomy which rendered her unable to show or feel emotions, like love.

It is debatable whether the real Frances Farmer actually received a lobotomy, but that procedure was widely used in those days for people, mostly women, who were deemed too "willful." The last scene of the film is a sad reunion between Frances and Harry where Harry realizes that Frances will never be able to express the love she once had for him. He says goodbye to her for the last time. The film's closing epilogue states: "Frances made one final movie *The Party Crashers*, and then moved to Indianapolis where she hosted a daytime television show *Frances Farmer Presents*. She died on August 1, 1970, at the age of 56. Harry was not with her. She died as she had lived... alone."

Jessica Lange and Kim Stanley were nominated for seven awards, including being nominated for Academy Awards and Golden Globe

Awards. Sam Shepard also did an excellent job on this film. Jessica Lange and Sam Shepard fell in love while working on the movie and subsequently had two children together. Speaking of children, my beautiful daughter Danielle was born during the filming of this movie. She was three months premature and has special needs. (I share this here only because I will be mentioning other things about her later.)

This was the first film Graeme Clifford directed. He was formerly an editor. He edited the film *The Postman Always Rings Twice,* which of course also starred Jessica Lange. There were some other big-name actors and future big-name actors in the movie. Anjelica Huston, who was also in *The Postman Always Rings Twice,* had a small part as a mental patient in the insane asylum.

This was one of Kevin Costner's first films. He had a very small un-credited part as "the man in the alley." I would later work on a Kevin Costner film, but I also worked with Kevin before he got his big start. Years before, Kevin worked as a stage manager at a small independent studio in Hollywood. Whenever I would work there on different commercials, I would call him to order lights and other equipment and he would deliver them to the stage. He, of course, did not remember me when I worked with him later, but I remembered him.

Frances – The Cast & Crew

Jessica Lange
(Photo Credit: Public Domain)

The Crew
(Photo by Carol McCullough)

THE TOY (1982)

Starring:	Richard Pryor, Jackie Gleason, Ned Beatty, Scott Schwartz, Teresa Ganzel, Wilfrid Hyde-White
Director:	Richard Donner
Cinematographer:	Laszlo Kovacs
Lighting Gaffer:	Aggie Aguilar
Best Boy:	Paul Caven (screen credit)

We filmed this movie in and around Baton Rouge, Louisiana, from April through June 1982. This was my first show with Dick Donner, and he quickly became one of my favorite directors. He is down to earth and an excellent director. The screenplay was written by Carol Sobieski, who also wrote *Casey's Shadow.* This was my second film with Ned Beatty, the first being *Deliverance.* He did not want to be reminded about *Deliverance* because of the rape scene, but he dropped his pants in this show too. Speaking of dropping your pants, Scott Schwartz (who was 14 years old when we filmed this movie) became a porn star later in his career; it was a short career.

Richard Pryor was fun to work with. This was before he caught himself on fire free-basing cocaine. One day while we were shooting the big outdoor party scene, Richard decided to have some fun. He grabbed a half a dozen balloons and tied a $100.00 bill to each one and let them go one at a time. That is just the kind of guy he was.

The biggest disappointment of my career was working with Jackie Gleason. When I found out that he was in this movie, I thought this was going to be wonderful working with "The Great One," as it says on the back of his director's chair. Unfortunately, I thought he was a great big jerk!

Gleason never knew his lines; he would ad-lib them, and then get angry at poor Scott when the little kid could not pick up his cue line because Jackie was ad-libbing everything. He was a chain smoker, and when he finished a cigarette, he would just drop it where ever he was,

143

on a carpet or anywhere. He would then shout, "Mel!", and his man servant Mel had to take care of the cigarette butt, put a new cigarette between his two outstretched fingers and light it. Mel had been with him for many years and was about the same age as Jackie Gleason. I assume he was very well paid. He was a very proper gentleman.

Jackie's wife Marilyn was a sweet person, and she was with him every day on the set. She was friendly and charming to everyone. She was an actress and had a small part in this film. I would like to think that when "The Great One" finally died of lung cancer in 1987, she and poor Mel got together and lived the high life the rest of their lives on Jackie Gleason's money.

Wilfrid Hyde-White had more class in his little finger than Jackie Gleason had in his whole body. Wilfrid was a class act. He was best known for his character Colonel Pickering in *My Fair Lady*. He was a real pro and an absolute gentleman. This would be one of his last movies.

The director, Dick Donner, gave himself a small speaking part in the film also. He was the guy who saw Richard and Scott breaking into the news office and then called the police.

As I mentioned before, my daughter Danielle was born a few months earlier that year. She was still in the NICU when I had to leave for location on this film. She was due to be released on Mother's Day weekend. Dick Donner, Richard Pryor and the crew pitched in to buy me a round-trip ticket back to Los Angeles so I could help bring Danielle home. Dick also sent flowers to Denise for Mother's Day. It was an incredible kindness that my family and I appreciated very much. It demonstrates how being on a movie crew is like being part of a family. They all knew how much I wanted to be there to help Denise, so they all pitched in.

The Toy – The Cast

Ned Beatty

Richard Pryor

Scott Schwartz & Richard Pryor

145

The Toy – The Crew

Foster Denker, Jonathan O'Neil, Aggie Aguilar, Laszlo Kovacs

Scott Schwartz & Richard Donner

Lunch Site

146

STAR 80 (1982)

Starring:	Mariel Hemingway, Eric Roberts, Cliff Robertson, Carroll Baker
Director:	Bob Fosse
Cinematographer:	Sven Nykvist
Lighting Gaffer:	Aggie Aguilar
Best Boy:	Paul Caven

We filmed this movie from August through September of 1982 in and around Los Angeles. They filmed some of the early scenes in Vancouver, Canada, Dorothy Stratten's hometown, but I did not work on that part. This was a disturbing true story about the life and murder of Playboy Playmate of the Year, Dorothy Stratten. It is a spellbinding drama about seduction and obsession. Paul Snider (played by Eric Roberts), a sleazy small-time hustler, seduces the beautiful Dorothy Stratten (played by Mariel Hemingway) as a young high school senior in Vancouver with the promise of making her a star in Hollywood. They get married and later he arranges an introduction for her to Hugh Hefner (played by Cliff Robertson), who puts her in Playboy Magazine.

Dorothy goes on to be a Playmate of the Year and starred in a few Hollywood movies, and in the process, leaves Paul Snider behind. Her last movie was directed by a character they call Aram Nicholas, who in reality was Peter Bogdanovich. Aram and Dorothy have an affair, and Paul Snider soon realizes that he is now out of the picture. In the final scene Paul Snider, in a fit of passion, rapes and brutally murders Dorothy and then commits suicide.

Eric Roberts and Mariel Hemingway did such a realistically haunting performance in the last scene that it was very difficult to watch as we were filming it. I have mentioned before, how it can be upsetting to have to stand there and witness such a realistic performance live. It is like watching a real murder take place right before your eyes and not being able to do anything about it. It can be very disturbing. The other ominous thing was the fact that we filmed the exteriors and some of the interiors (although not the murder scene) at their real apartment where the actual murder took place two years before. It was creepy!

Eric Roberts was nominated for a Golden Globe Award and won the Boston Society of Film Critic's Award. Mariel Hemingway was a sweet person and did a wonderful job in a very difficult role. Hugh Hefner's younger brother, Keith Hefner, had a small part in the film but Hugh Hefner sued Warner Brothers because he did not like the way he was portrayed.

Bob Fosse was a remarkable person to work with. Known more, of course, as a brilliant choreographer, he also directed such classic movies as *Sweet Charity, Cabaret,* and *All That Jazz.* Regrettably, he passed away five years after this film at the age of 60. He had a reputation of being driven and demanding, but that was not the Bob Fosse we saw. In a lot of ways, I think he thought of himself as one of the crew. We used to razz him because he always wore black levis and a black (usually silk) shirt. We teased saying we were going to make a million dollars marketing a Bob Fosse "the man in black" line of clothing. He got a real kick out of that and a big laugh.

My wife Denise brought our daughter Danielle to the set one day for lunch. Many of the people on this show also worked on *Frances* and *The Toy,* so they knew about Danielle and were excited to see her at last. This was Danielle's first trip to the set; she was about 8 months old. After lunch, we were walking up the steps to the set when Bob Fosse came bounding up behind us (he never walked anywhere). When he reached us, he said, "Where's this little girl I've been hearing so much about?" He took Danielle from my arms, held her, and gave her a gentle little kiss on her cheek, handed her back to me, gave us a big smile and ran off. He had a sensitivity that few people got to see.

This was another film we worked on with cinematographer Sven Nykvist. He was such a wonderful person and an extraordinarily sensitive artist. He was a soft-spoken and gentle person with a quiet, dry sense of humor accompanied by a subtle, contagious little smile that one could not resist.

Star 80 – The Cast

Paul:
You look like
you should be in
the mountains but
I am glad you were, are
working here.
Thanx

Love
Mariel —:

**Mariel Hemingway's Good
Wishes**

THE GRACE KELLY STORY (1982)

Starring:	Cheryl Ladd, Lloyd Bridges, Diane Ladd, Alejandro Rey, Ian McShane
Director:	Anthony Page
Cinematographer:	Woody Omens
Lighting Gaffer:	Aggie Aguilar
Best Boy:	Paul Caven *(screen credit)*

This was a made for TV movie and obviously a biography of Grace Kelly. It chronicles her rise from a Philadelphia socialite, to movie star, to Princess of Monaco. The story recounts the former Hollywood star's crisis of marriage and identity, during a political dispute between Monaco's Prince Rainier III and France's Charles De Gaulle, and a looming French invasion of Monaco in the early 1960s. Some of it, of course, was filmed in Monaco, but we only worked on the filming in Los Angeles and at the RMS Queen Mary in Long Beach in the fall of 1982.

Cheryl Ladd was very pleasant and very friendly with the crew. She had just finished a four-year run on the highly successful TV show *Charlie's Angel's*. It was wonderful working with Lloyd Bridges and Alejandro Rey—both old pros and fun to be around. This was one of the first films for Christina Applegate. She played the young Grace Kelly. She was about 11 years old at the time.

The Grace Kelly Story – The Cast

Cheryl Ladd's Good Wishes

SWING SHIFT (1983)

Starring:	Goldie Hawn, Kurt Russell, Christine Lahti, Ed Harris, Fred Ward, Holly Hunter
Director:	Jonathan Demme
Cinematographer:	Tak Fujimoto
Lighting Gaffer:	Mel Maxwell
Best Boy:	Paul Caven *(*screen credit)

This was the only movie I ever did with this gaffer, Mel Maxwell. He had worked with Aggie on *Easy Rider,* so when he was looking for a best boy for this film he called Aggie. We were between shows at the time so Aggie suggested me. This was also the only show I ever did with the cameraman, Tak Fujimoto. Tak did a great job on this film. He had worked mostly on TV shows but later he did such movies as *Ferris Bueller's Day Off,* and *Silence of the Lambs.*

We filmed this movie around the Los Angeles area from February through May of 1983. We filmed exteriors at Fort MacArthur in San Pedro, The Long Beach Naval Base, The Huntington Hotel, Pasadena, and Santa Monica. The interiors and the exterior of the bungalows where they lived were on stage at Warner Brothers Studio. They built that entire exterior set on stage including the street, the sidewalk and all the palm trees.

The movie was about a young married couple (Goldie Hawn and Ed Harris) whose lives are changed forever when he volunteers for the Navy after the attack on Pearl Harbor in 1941. She gets a job on the swing shift building war planes in an airplane factory. She becomes friends with one of her neighbors in the bungalow court (Christine Lahti) who also works at the factory. She reluctantly becomes even better friends with one of her bosses (Kurt Russell), who moonlights as a trumpet player in a band. They eventually have an affair, which comes to an abrupt end when her husband comes home from the war. He ends up forgiving her, and they get back together and live happily ever after.

This was the first movie in which Goldie Hawn and Kurt Russell worked together, and they have been together ever since. Christine Lahti was nominated for an Academy Award and a Golden Globe Award for best supporting actress, as well as winning the New York Film Critics Award and a second place by the Los Angeles Film Critics. Goldie's mother, Laura Hawn, had a part as Ethel, one of the people living in the bungalow court. Chris Lemmon, Jack Lemmon's son, also had a small part. Roger Corman, the legendary producer of low budget 'B' movies, played the part of the owner of the factory. The original script was written by Nancy Dowd and then rewritten by others. When the film was released, the writing credit was assigned to the fictional "Rob Morton"... don't ask me!

Swing Shift - The Shooting Crew

The Shooting Crew
(Photo Credit: John Shannon)

THIS GIRL FOR HIRE (1983)

Starring:	Bess Armstrong, Celeste Holm, Cliff De Young, Hermione Baddeley, Scott Brady, Howard Duff, Jose` Ferrer, Beverly Garland, Roddy McDowall, Percy Rodrigues, Ray Walston, Elisha Cook, William Lanteau
Director:	Jerry Jameson
Cinematographer:	Robbie Greenberg
Lighting Gaffer:	Aggie Aguilar
Best Boy:	Paul Caven (screen credit)

We filmed this TV Pilot for twelve days in June of 1983. We filmed in and around Los Angeles including Grauman's Chinese Theater and Union Station. It was our only show with Robbie Greenberg. Years later he would be the cinematographer on the original *Free Willy*. We would do *Free Willy-2*. In this pilot for a proposed TV series, B.T. Brady (played by Bess Armstrong) is a flippant and somewhat klutzy female private detective in Hollywood who sets out to solve the murder of an obnoxious mystery writer. Along the way, Brady gets help from her flamboyant mother Zandra (played by Celeste Holm) a washed-up actress, as well as Brady's live-in boyfriend Wolfe (played by Howard Duff) who runs a Hollywood memorabilia shop. It had an all-star cast; it just did not sell. But the lighting was great!

THE WOMAN IN RED (1983)

Starring:	Gene Wilder, Charles Grodin, Joseph Bologna, Judith Ivey, Michael Huddleston, Kelly LeBrock, Gilda Radner
Director:	Gene Wilder
Cinematographer:	Fred Schuler
Lighting Gaffer:	Aggie Aguilar
Best Boy:	Paul Caven *(*screen credit)

We filmed this movie from October to December of 1983. Some of it was filmed in LA but the majority of it was filmed in San Francisco. The working title was, *Boys Will Be Boys.* Gene Wilder plays a middle-aged man named Teddy Pierce. He has a good wife, kids, friends and a fine job. You could say that he has everything he wants; but he doesn't. One day on his way to work he sees a gorgeous woman in a red dress, and goes crazy! He must have her.

Gene Wilder was the director as well as being the main actor. He was a fun guy to work with. He and Gilda Radner met on a film before this called *Hanky Panky.* However, Gilda was married at the time to a musician on *Saturday Night Live.* They divorced in 1982. She and Gene fell in love on this movie and were married a year later. They were made for each other; they both had a great sense of humor. Gilda was best known for her five years on *Saturday Night Live.* She apparently was the first person cast on the new SNL show when it first started.

The whole crew loved Gilda, but we used to joke about the little dog that she carried everywhere on the set. It was a little Yorkie or something like that. We used to call it "the dog with no legs" because she never put it down on the ground; Gilda carried it all the time. Gilda was diagnosed with cancer and passed away five years after this show at the age of 42.

The rest of the cast were all experienced actors except for Kelly LeBrock. At the age of 23, this was Kelly's first film. I think she did a good job with a very difficult part for a young actress. She lost her

155

father a few years earlier and Gene Wilder became a surrogate father to her. She remained friends with Gene and Gilda until Gene's passing in 2016. Stevie Wonder produced all the music on the film and performed some of it with Dionne Warwick. He received an Academy Award and a Golden Globe for Best Music for the song "I Just Called to Say I Love You." Charles Grodin was fun to work with. He plays one of Teddy's good friends. Speaking of good friends, while we were filming, a couple of my good friends came to visit the set at a Rolls Royce dealership.

Throughout my career, I had the occasional opportunity to invite friends to observe some of the production of films I worked on. In this film I was able to invite two friends who lived in San Francisco at the time to join us on the set at the local Rolls Royce dealership. They arrived and the assistant director told them to stand in the back and to stay quiet. They had the chance to observe the lighting being set for the scene we were about to shoot. It took a while to get the lighting right for a short scene in which Charles Grodin was to drive a Rolls Royce into the dealership showroom. We finally got all the lighting ready, and then the director, Gene Wilder, came on set. After a quick rehearsal, he called "Action" and Charles Grodin took only 20 seconds to drive the car into position, and then Wilder called "Cut." As my friends were watching, at the end of that scene, in the silence after we cut, I just kind of blurted out "All this just for that?" Everyone could hear the comment and they all had a good chuckle. My friends remind me of their visit to the set every time I see them and they remember that experience with a smile and a laugh to this day.

The Woman In Red – The Cast

Gene Wilder

Kelly LeBrock

The Woman In Red – The Crew

Horse Stunt

The Crew Shooting

The Crew
(Photo Credit: Sidney Baldwin)

157

IT CAME UPON A MIDNIGHT CLEAR (1984)

Starring:	Mickey Rooney, Scott Grimes, Barrie Youngfellow, Elisha Cook and George Gaynes
Director:	Peter Hunt
Cinematographer:	Dean Cundey
Lighting Gaffer:	Pat Marshall

This was a TV Christmas movie that we filmed in April of 1984. It was weird shooting Christmas tree lots and houses with Christmas lights on them in April. They filmed some of this show in New York, but I only worked on the part they filmed in Los Angeles. It is one of my favorite Christmas movies. It is sweet, funny and sad and brings out the joy of Christmas in us all. They don't play it at Christmas anymore and it's hard to find a copy of it.

This was one of Scott Grimes' first movies, he was 12 years old. This was my third film with the great character actor George Gaynes. I worked with him on *Harry and Walter Go to New York* and *Nickelodeon*. Another great character actor on this show was Elisha Cook, who I had just worked with the year before on another TV movie, *This Girl for Hire.*

Mickey Rooney was wonderful to work with, but I guess it was not always that way. Apparently, when he was a child actor, he was pretty obnoxious. As a matter of fact, there is a camera move named after him. In the old days, when a cameraman wanted the camera dolly to creep very slowly from one spot to another, he would say to his crew, "Just do a Mickey Rooney from here to there," meaning a little creep. All I know is he was very friendly to us.

There are many phrases like "Do a Mickey Rooney" that are unique to the movie business. Sometimes a cameraman will ask an actor to "Do a banana." What he wants them to do is to walk a curved line from point A to point B, curving away from the camera rather than a straight line from point A to point B to make it easier to keep focus. A cameraman will sometimes ask an actor to "Do a Groucho." That means that he wants them to crouch down a little as they cross camera so the camera man does not have to tilt the camera up and possibly see off the top of the set as they pass camera. The cameraman may ask the gaffer to bring in an "Obie Light." Obie is short for Merle Oberon, a

158

famous actress in the 1930s. In 1937, she was in an automobile accident in England which left her face scarred. After the accident, she resumed her career. Her husband, Lucien Ballard, a camera man, used a light that would soften the scarring on her face, a flat fill light directly above the camera lens - thus the Obie light is short for Oberon.

When it is the second to the last shot of the day the assistant director will announce, "This shot is the Abby Singer." Abby Singer was a notorious production manager at Universal Studios years ago. He would come to the set at the end of the day to hurry things up, and when it came to the second to the last shot, he would start getting the crew to wrap things up and get ready for a wrap so they could get off the clock faster. On the last shot of the day, the assistant director would announce, "OK boys and girls this is the 'Martini shot'." Meaning after this shot you can have a martini, or in our case, a wrap beer. I had my own little phrase that I would say to my crew at wrap time. I would say, "OK boys and girls let's wrap this up pronto, I've got a cold drink and a hot woman waiting at home and the situation is rapidly reversing!"

Sometimes a director wants to do a shot without sound. The assistant director would announce, "This shot will be MOS." That acronym comes from the director Otto Preminger who when he wanted to shoot without sound would say in his thick Hungarian accent, "Ve vill shoot Mit Out Sound"... MOS.

It Came Upon a Midnight Clear – The Cast

Mickey Rooney's Good Wishes

159

MASK (1984)

Starring: Cher, Sam Elliot, Eric Stoltz

Director: Peter Bogdanovich

Cinematographer: Laszlo Kovacs

Lighting Gaffer: Aggie Aguilar

Best Boy: Paul Caven (screen credit)

We filmed this movie in the summer of 1984 around the Los Angeles area, including the Azusa neighborhood where Rocky (played by Eric Stoltz) and Rusty Dennis (played by Cher) actually lived. As a matter of fact, while we were shooting in the neighborhood, we met several people who knew the real Rocky. The real Rusty Dennis came on the set a few times. She died several years later in a motorcycle accident.

This was my fifth and last movie with Peter Bogdanovich. This was his first movie in the four years after the death of his girlfriend Dorothy Stratten, as documented in the movie *Star 80*. This film, of course, fit into Peter's mold of long master shots and long depth of field. Peter wanted to use Bruce Springsteen music for the background music. Not only because he felt Springsteen music fit the movie better, but it was the real Rocky's favorite music. Universal Studios could not come to an agreement with Bruce's record company, so they insisted on Bob Seger music instead. Twenty years later Peter was able to release a "Director's Cut" version of the show with several added scenes that the studio had cut and with Bruce Springsteen music.

This show had a great cast. Sam Elliot was as cool as you would think. He is just an everyday cowboy with a million dollar smile (and that voice!). Cher was really friendly. She won the Best Actress Award at the Cannes Film Festival for this film. I think she never looked more beautiful due to the way Laszlo photographed her and how Aggie lit her. Peter also used his old friend Harry Carey Jr. who had worked on *"Nickelodeon."*

Dennis Burkley plays a biker named Dozer on the show who has a speech impediment; he stutters. Peter, as I have mentioned before, likes to give actors a challenge. Well, all I know is, he has only given an actor the challenge of stuttering twice, and they were both on shows I worked on with Peter... I'm just sayin'.

Laura Dern did a fabulous job playing a very convincing blind girl in this film. I worked with her father, Bruce Dern. on *King of Marvin Gardens*. She worked so hard at not focusing her eyes that she later had eye problems. She plays Rocky's love interest. Because she is blind and does not see his deformed face, she falls in love with the Rocky within. He meets her while he is working at a summer camp for children who are blind. We filmed at an actual camp, Camp Bloomfield, in the Santa Monica Mountains above Malibu, using a lot of the real campers.

It was really fun working with the kids. There were not only blind kids but also deaf kids. They were all, of course, very interested in us and wanted to know everything about us. One day I was talking to some of the deaf kids, and they all started looking at each other with curious looks on their faces. I did not know what was going on. It turned out that because of my stutter, they were having a hard time reading my lips. I got a real laugh out of that and told them I would start talking slower and try not to stutter.

In the film, we show the blind kids playing baseball. It was really cool how they adapted the game so the blind kids could play. They used a dodge ball, and the pitcher would roll it towards home plate. They placed a strip of tin foil about three feet in front of home plate so when the kid heard the ball cross the tin foil, they knew to swing the bat. When they got a hit, a person at first base would ring a bell so they knew to run towards the bell. It was really fun to watch, and the kids had a great time.

Eric Stoltz did an unbelievable job on this film. Why he did not get an Academy Award for this role, I will never know. Michael Westmore, of the legendary family of Westmore make-up artists, and Zoltan Elek won the very first Academy Award given for make-up for this movie. Michael created the look and Zoltan applied it every day. The only un-made-up part of Eric's face was his lower lip and his eyes, but the emotions he expressed with his eyes were extraordinary. It was a grueling four-and-a-half-hour make-up procedure every morning and another couple of hours to remove it at night. Because of the time it took, none of us ever really saw the real "Eric Stoltz." He came in before any of the crew, and we were all gone before he was through at night. Because of that, this was the only show I ever worked on that the crew never called an actor by his name. We all called Eric 'Rocky' on the set. It was extraordinary. I have never seen that happen before or after that. As a matter of fact, when Eric showed up at the wrap party, nobody knew who he was. He, of course, knew all of us, so he had to go around and introduce himself.

In the script, Rocky reads a poem he wrote to Rusty. The poem was a poem that the real Rocky actually wrote, it goes:

"These things are good: ice cream and cake, a ride on a Harley, seeing monkeys in the trees, the rain on my tongue, and the sun shining on my face.

These things are a drag: dust in my hair, holes in my shoes, no money in my pocket, and the sun shining on my face."

When Harry Carey Jr's character dies in the film, Rocky has a line saying he is "everywhere now." When Rocky dies, Rusty looks at the map of Europe showing all the places he was planning to tour some day and says, "You can go anywhere now, baby." That line gets to me every time.

This show was a marvelous experience to work on and is a timeless classic. If you have never seen it, make a point to see it you will not be disappointed!

QUICKSILVER (1984-85)

Starring:	Kevin Bacon, Jami Gertz, Paul Rodriguez, Rudy Ramos, Laurence Fishburne, Louie Anderson
Director/Writer:	Thomas Michael Donnelly
Cinematographer:	Thomas Del Ruth
Lighting Gaffer:	Aggie Aguilar, Danny Buck
1st *Best Boy:*	Paul Caven (screen credit)

We filmed this movie from November 1984 through January 1985 in San Francisco, Los Angeles and at Warner Brothers Studio. This was a cute little film that did not really do very well at the box office. The story was about Jack Casey (played by Kevin Bacon) who is a big shot stock broker who loses it all one day. He becomes a bicycle messenger and is enjoying the free life when he decides to go back to the stock exchange one more time just to help a friend (played by Paul Rodriguez). He strikes it rich again. Jack falls in love with fellow messenger Terri (played by Jami Gertz) and saves her from the bad guy. There is a lot of trick bike riding, fast bike riding, great music and a pretty good car/bicycle chase but it just did not go over.

We filmed the scenes in the stock exchange at the San Francisco Stock Exchange. That was an eye-opener for me. I stood there watching these groups of people shouting at each other, buying and selling little strips of paper, and realized that this is what our economy is being based on. The deals these people are making, or not making, affect our national economy and my IRA... God help us!

Tom Del Ruth was a cameraman that neither Aggie nor I had worked with before. We got the job because the key grip, our friend Gene Kearney, recommended us to him. Apparently, his regular gaffer (Danny Buck) was not available when the show started. After a few weeks of shooting, Danny became available, so Tom Del Ruth started bad mouthing Aggie saying they were not getting along and that he and Aggie had different concepts for lighting. Aggie ended up getting fired, and Danny Buck was hired along with his best boy Don Bixby and his crew.

They fired my crew right before Christmas. They kept me on as Best Boy to tend to all of Aggie's equipment that was rented to the company for the run of the show. Needless to say, I did not get along very well with Danny Buck or Tom Del Ruth. One day we were shooting in an office building downtown. I was working in the truck when Danny called me on the walkie-talkie and told me to come upstairs. When I got there, he told me he wanted me to change all the florescent tubes in one of the offices we were going to shoot. I informed him, "I was not hired as your extra man, I was hired to make sure you don't steal anything so, if you need extra help, I suggest you have your best boy call the local." I went back down to the truck. I got along alright though with Don Bixby; as a matter of fact, I ended up working for Don many years later when he became a gaffer.

Quicksilver – The Cast

Kevin Bacon

Paul Rodriguez & Kevin Bacon

SHADOW CHASERS (1985)

Starring: Trevor Eve, Dennis Dugan

Director: Various Directors

Cinematographer: Michael Margulies

This was a Warner Brothers TV show that we filmed from September to November of 1985. This was kind of a quirky show about a sleazy scandal-sheet reporter, played by Dennis Dugan, and a stiff British college professor, played by Trevor Eve, who team up to investigate UFO sightings, vampires, time-travelers, ghosts and other paranormal mysteries. I had worked with Dennis Dugan 10 years earlier on *Harry and Walter Go to New York.* The problem with working on a TV show like this is that everyone knows UFO's, vampires, ghosts, and other paranormal mysteries only happen at night, so we worked a lot of nights and when we work at night we use a lot more lights. The show was not very good; it only lasted one season.

On Halloween night, we were filming in a house in Glendale, California. The subject matter of the show being what it was, meant the prop man had a coffin in his truck. He set it up on the front lawn of the house we were shooting in, and we put scary lights on it. The make-up artist made up one of the drivers to look like the walking dead, and we put him in the coffin with a walkie-talkie. Whenever any trick-or-treaters came to look at the casket, we would cue the guy in the coffin on the walkie-talkie, and he would throw open the casket lid and scare the bejesus out of the kids… they loved it! The prop guy would then give all the kids candy.

LEGAL EAGLES (1986)

Starring:	Robert Redford, Debra Winger, Daryl Hannah
Director:	Ivan Reitman
Cinematographer:	Laszlo Kovacs
Lighting Gaffer:	Aggie Aguilar
Best Boy:	Paul Caven (screen credit)

District Attorney Tom Logan (played by Robert Redford) is set for higher office, until he becomes involved with defense lawyer Laura Kelly (played by Debra Winger) and her unpredictable client Chelsea Deardon (played by Daryl Hannah). It seems the least of Chelsea's crimes is the theft of a very valuable painting. The women persuade Logan to investigate further as a much more sinister scenario starts to emerge. The thing I remember most about this film is "Fire." We had a lot of fire; burning buildings, burning offices, and burning art galleries; we even had a special effects guy accidently catch his sleeve on fire. I hate fire!

They filmed some of the exterior scenes in New York, but our crew did not do the New York filming. We picked the show up in Los Angeles. We filmed from January to March of 1986 in and around Los Angeles, on Warner Brothers ranch lot and Universal Studios back lot, as well as a few stages at Universal.

This was my second and last show with Robert Redford. He was nice to work with and very friendly. Debra Winger did a great job on this show and was really lovely, too. Daryl Hannah was very pleasant as well. Ivan Reitman was not one of my favorite directors; he was not very friendly with the crew.

Legal Eagles – The Cast

Robert Redford's Good Wishes

NUTS (1986)

Starring:	Barbra Streisand, Richard Dreyfuss, Maureen Stapleton, Karl Malden, Eli Wallach, Robert Webber, James Whitmore, Leslie Nielsen
Director:	Martin Ritt
Cinematographer:	Andrzej Bartkowiak
Lighting Gaffer:	Chris Strong

Chris Strong had worked with Aggie and me on several films and had just started gaffing. He hired me for the Los Angeles shooting. I did not care for the cameraman, he was rather disagreeable. He had to keep hiring new, inexperienced gaffers because he could not get the more experienced gaffers to work with him. I worked October and November of 1986. We filmed mostly on stage at The Burbank Studios (Warner Brothers)

This was my third show with Barbra Streisand. I had worked with Maureen Stapleton eight years before on *The Runner Stumbles.* I worked on the first season of *The Streets of San Francisco* with Karl Malden. This was my only film with Richard Dreyfuss. He is an Academy Award winning actor and did an incredible job on this show. I had worked with Leslie Nielsen a few times on various TV series and just five years earlier on *Wrong is Right.* I had worked with the Director Marty Ritt before on *Casey's Shadow.* He was very pleasant and an excellent Director.

LITTLE NIKITA (1987)

Starring: Sidney Poitier, River Phoenix, Richard Jenkins, Caroline Kava, Richard Bradford, Richard Lynch

Director: Richard Benjamin

Cinematographer: Laszlo Kovacs

Lighting Gaffer: Aggie Aguilar

Best Boy: Paul Caven (screen credit)

We filmed this movie from January to April of 1987. We filmed mostly in San Diego, but the nursery/house and the house across the street were in Monrovia, California, and all the interiors were filmed on stage at Warner Brothers. I thought this was an ok movie; not great but ok. I felt the story was a little weak. It is about an FBI agent named Roy Parmenter, played by Sidney Poitier. Agent Parmenter interviews an applicant to the Air Force Academy named Jeff Grant, played by River Phoenix. During a routine background check, Roy discovers that Jeff's parents, played by Richard Jenkins and Caroline Kava, are Russian sleeper spies. He has to find out if Jeff is also a spy. During his investigation he discovers that Jeff is unaware of his parent's secret life and that his parents are being hunted by other Russian spies who want to kill them. Roy must confront Jeff's parents and protect them from the other Russian Spies. It is a real cat and mouse story.

It was not known at the time, but many years later it was revealed that there was a cell of Russian Sleeper agents who had been "hiding in plain sight" in the United States for decades. Several of them had children, coworkers, friends, and neighbors who all had no idea that they were spies. In 2010, a group of these so-called "Illegals" were arrested and ultimately returned to Russia in a trade for some Americans that Russia was holding. I guess the story was not so weak.

I felt the directing was a little amateurish, but it had its moments. I liked Richard Benjamin; he was very charming, and a good actor. We worked with him as an actor on *How to Beat the High Cost of living*, but I did not think he was a very good director. It was, of course, a thrill to work with the Academy Award winning actor Sidney Poitier. He was really friendly. River Phoenix was 16 years old when we filmed this show. He was a good clean-cut kid, but at the age of 23 he fell, in a drunken stupor on the way out of a Hollywood night club, and hit his head on the pavement, and died on the spot. What a waste of a young life. I would work with Richard Jenkins 20 years later on *Six Feet Under.*

SUNSET (1987)

Starring:	Bruce Willis, James Garner, Malcom McDowell, Mariel Hemingway, Kathleen Quinlan
Director:	Blake Edwards
Cinematographer:	Tony Richmond
Lighting Gaffer:	Foster Denker
Best Boy:	Paul Caven

Foster Denker was a friend who had worked with Aggie and me on many shows. He also worked with Aggie on *Easy Rider.* When he asked me to do the show, I told him I would do it, but I was finishing up *Little Nikita* with Aggie and would not be able to start the show. I told him I could join the show in a couple of weeks. Foster hired a friend of his, Larry Flynn, to start the show as best boy until I could join him. The funny part is that Larry received the best boy screen credit for the show even though he only worked the first couple of weeks of the show. That's show biz!

We filmed this movie from April through June of 1987. We filmed around Los Angeles, at Bell Ranch in Santa Susana, and Melody Ranch in Newhall, California, as well as Culver City Studio. The train scenes were filmed in Perris, California, at the Orange Empire Railroad Museum, and the final scenes were filmed on a ranch near San Jose, California.

This was my only film with Bruce Willis, and I must say I was not very impressed. It was all pretty much about him. He got first billing over the more veteran professional actor James Garner. In James Garner's autobiography: *You Ought to be in Pictures*, he wrote: "I'd never work with Bruce Willis again. I did that Blake Edwards film with him, *Sunset*. Willis is high school. He's not that serious about his work. He thinks he's so clever he can just walk through it, make up dialogue and stuff. I don't think you work that way." This, once again, is a clear example of the difference between the old school actors and the young turks. Jim Garner was a pro. Bruce Willis's attitude always reminds me of my favorite Peter O'Toole line in the great movie *My Favorite Year,* he says, "I'm not an actor, I'm a movie star!"

I had worked with James Garner years before on his TV series *Nichols* at Warner Brothers and worked with him again later on *My Fellow Americans.* Jim was a joy to work with. I had worked with Mariel Hemingway five years earlier on *Star 80.* She did an incredible job on that show, but I felt that her work on this show was a little weak. As a matter of fact, she was nominated for a Razzie Award for Worst Supporting Actress. I had also worked with Kathleen Quinlan before on *The Runner Stumbles.* Kathleen was one of my favorite actresses and I think she did a good job on this film. It was a great character for her.

This was the only movie I worked on with the legendary writer/director Blake Edwards. However, I do not think his mind or heart was in this film. He won a Razzie Award for Worst Director. His producer on this film was my old buddy Tony Adams. You may remember me mentioning Tony working on *Deliverance* as a Nanny/Teacher for John Boorman's kids sixteen years earlier, and how we had Tony to our house for dinner after we got home from location. Tony apparently had amnesia about that period of his life, and he never acknowledged my presence on the film. You know how it goes: "What have you done for me lately?"

The critics did not like this film very much but I thought it was a good movie. Of course, we all know the value of my judgment. It did kind of stretch reality a little; but isn't that what movies do? It is all make-believe. Like what Jim Garner's character says at the end of the show when asked if the story was true, he replies, "It's the truth, give or take a lie or two."

Sunset – The Cast

James Garner

Bruce Willis

The Shootout

173

NERDS OF A FEATHER aka SPIES AND LOVERS (1988)

Starring:	Mario Romeo Milano, Kathleen Kickta, Patrick McCormick, Anya Karin, Charles Pierce, Peter Risch, Charles Dierkop
Director:	Gary Graver
Cinematographer:	Aggie Aguilar
Lighting Gaffer/ *Key Grip:*	Paul Caven and R. Michael Stringer

This was a low budget, non-union, wild and wooly, shoot from the hip, one man catastrophe. Mario Romeo Milano was not only the lead actor he was the writer, co-director, and producer, a jack of all trades and a master of none. Mercifully, he only did a couple of movies. This ended up being two bad movies. When we filmed the show, it was called *Nerds of a Feather.* Later on, they split it up and released a "sequel" called *Spies and Lovers.* Neither one made any money.

On this kind of film, the crew is pretty much interchangeable as far as the company is concerned. Aggie was the cameraman. I was hired and worked as the gaffer, and I received credit as the gaffer on *Nerds of a Feather,* but they gave me screen credit as the key grip on *Spies and Lovers.* Mike Stringer who was the key grip received credit as the gaffer on *Spies and Lovers.* Go figure.

SAY ANYTHING (1988)

Starring:	John Cusack, Ione Skye, John Mahoney
Director:	Cameron Crowe
Cinematographer:	Laszlo Kovacs
Lighting Gaffer:	Aggie Aguilar
Best Boy;	Paul Caven (screen credit)

Laszlo was asked to do this film by the producer Polly Platt. Polly was Peter Bogdanovich's ex-wife and had worked with us on several of Peter's movies, as a production designer, while they were still married. We all liked Polly a lot. We worked with her on *What's Up Doc?* and *Paper Moon.* She was a very creative and talented designer. She was the first female member of the Art Directors Guild. But she was the producer on this film and wanted Laszlo to do the film so that he could help the first time Director/Writer Cameron Crowe.

I have mentioned before that, in my experience and observation, writers do not make good directors because they usually do not know what to do with the camera. That is why Polly hired Laszlo. Cameron was an acclaimed writer, he wrote *Fast Times at Ridgemont High,* but this was his directing debut. Cameron was very low key, not your usual run of the mill Hollywood type. He went on to be an award-winning director for shows like *Jerry Maguire,* and *Almost Famous.* We broke him in!

John Cusack plays the un-ambitious teenager, Lloyd Dobler, who has a crush on the gorgeous bookworm Diane Court, played by Ione Skye. Lloyd decides to invite Diane to a high school graduation party and she accepts. Lloyd is living with his sister Constance, played by John's real sister Joan Cusack, and has no plan for his future. Diane lives with her father James Court, played by John Mahoney, who is the owner of a retirement home. She has just received a scholarship to a prestigious British college. Soon Lloyd and Diane fall in love. James Court is convicted of stealing money from the patients in his retirement home and is sent to prison. Diane decides to go to England anyway and Lloyd goes with her and they live happily ever after.

John Cusack was 22 years old when he made this film. I thought he did a marvelous job. I would work with him later in his career on *Midnight in the Garden of Good and Evil.* Ione Skye Leitch was 18 years old. Ione is the daughter of the 60s "flower child" singer Donovan Leitch. John Mahoney was a veteran actor. I would work with him again later on *Primal Fear.* He would later become better known for his role on the TV show *Fraser.*

Eric Stoltz, who we worked with on *Mask,* had a small part in this film, but worked the rest of the film as a production assistant. He said he wanted to experience what it was like to work behind the scenes...actors, go figure! It was great working with Eric when he was not in character as Rocky from *Mask* (as I noted before, we never knew the real Eric when we worked on *Mask).* Barbra Streisand and Elliot Gould's son, Jason Gould, had a small part in the party scene as Mike Cameron.

AN INNOCENT MAN (1989)

Starring:	Tom Selleck, F. Murray Abraham, Laila Robbins, Dennis Burkley
Director:	Peter Yates
Cinematographer:	William Fraker
Lighting Gaffer:	Gerald Boatright

We filmed this movie from January through April of 1989. The shooting title was *Hard Rain,* playing off of the Tom Selleck character's name, Jimmy Rainwood, but they changed the title to *An Innocent Man* before they released it because the Ridley Scott movie *Black Rain* with Michael Douglas was released first.

This was my first movie with this gaffer. I was hired by his best boy, Don Yamasaki, whom I had worked with before. I had worked with the director Peter Yates before on *For Pete's Sake* and I had worked with Dennis Burkley on *Mask.* F. Murray Abraham was a very nice person. He would hang out with us at night after work in the hotel bar.

I was thrilled to work with the celebrated cinematographer Bill Fraker. Fraker (everybody just called him Fraker) filmed some classic films such as: *Rosemary's Baby, Looking for Mr. Goodbar, Heaven Can Wait,* as well as working with Peter Yates on the groundbreaking film (with the best chase scene ever filmed) *Bullitt* with Steve McQueen. He filmed parts of the famous chase scene footage while strapped to the front of the Mustang going 100 mph. Fraker was very enjoyable and he had a wonderful sense of humor. He liked to keep it light on the set. He liked when the guys would joke around. He also enjoyed a little nip at the end of a long day. When they called the "Abbey Singer" shot each night, his camera assistant would bring the "special" camera case on the set. The case was set up to be a mini-mini bar. He would open the case, pour himself a drink, sit back in his chair and wait for them to say "Wrap." He was a classic! One of a kind!

We filmed in various places in the Los Angeles area, San Pedro (the house was in San Pedro), and Long Beach. The exterior prison scenes were filmed at the Nevada State Prison in Carson City, Nevada. It was a working prison, so we had to conform to all the prison security regulations. This meant that we were not allowed to bring in our tools; we were not allowed to wear Levis jeans or denim shirts either because that was what the prisoners wear. We were also told the same thing we were told at the Ohio State Prison, that if we were out in the yard and heard the alarm or gun shots, to "hit the ground, don't run, because anyone not on the ground will be shot."

The interior prison scenes were filmed at the old Hamilton County Jail in Cincinnati, Ohio. The jail, also known as the "Cincinnati Workhouse," had been permanently closed. It was built during the Civil War to house rebel troops and was still in use by Hamilton County and Cincinnati area police agencies as a jail as late as the 1970s. It was closed due to being "inhumane, cruel and unusual punishment" by modern jail standards.

I was not very impressed with Tom Selleck. Let's just say I was not a fan. He was not very friendly with the crew, at least not with the male members of the crew. We filmed for a few days at the gymnasium of Norwood High School in Norwood, Ohio. It was supposed to be the prison gym. During lunch, a bunch of us would go into the school gym and play a little basketball. One day we were in there playing when one of the production assistants came in and told us we had to vacate the gym because Tom wanted to come in and shoot some hoops by himself. Not very cool!

An Innocent Man – The Crew

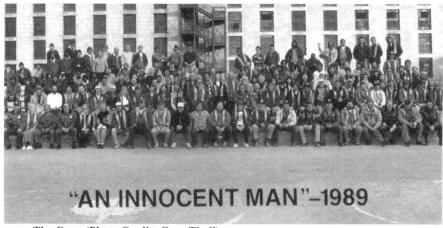

The Crew (Photo Credit: Gene Tindl)

TANGO AND CASH (1989)

Starring: Sylvester Stallone, Kurt Russell, Terri Hatcher, Jack Palance, Brion James, James Hong, Michael J. Pollard, Geoffrey Lewis

Director: Andrei Konchalovsky, Albert Magnoli

Cinematographer: Barry Sonnenfeld, Donald E. Thorin

Lighting Gaffer: James Boyle

Second Unit Director: Peter MacDonald

*Second Unit
Cinematographer:*   Julio Macat

*Second Unit
Lighting Gaffer:*   Gerald Boatright

I was a lamp operator on the second unit of this film. A second (shooting) unit is basically used to shoot stunt scenes and scenes that do not involve the principal actors. We filmed the second unit in July and August of 1989. The first unit was plagued with problems. They fired the Director, Stallone fired the cameraman, and, when the studio did not like the first cut, they hired a new editor to re-edit it. They even changed the title; it was originally titled *The Set Up.* That is probably why this film was nominated for a Razzie Award for Worst Actor - Sylvester Stallone, Worst Supporting Actress - Kurt Russell (in drag), and Worst Screenplay - Randy Feldman. The story was weak and implausible.

This was my second movie in a row with Jerry Boatright. I liked Jerry; he was a very polite guy and a good gaffer. This was my first movie with Julio Macat. I was not impressed. I would work with Julio a couple more times, however, with mixed results (we will get into that later). This was my second movie with Kurt Russell having worked with him on *Swing Shift.*

We filmed the escape sequence at the Ohio State Prison at

179

Mansfield, Ohio, the same prison where we filmed *Harry and Walter Go to New York* 14 years earlier. We had some of the same prison lifer trustees working with us on both films. The escape scene takes place during a rain storm. You cannot rely on Mother Nature to rain when you need it so the special effects crew had to create rain. The effects crew set up huge sprinkler rigs hung on cranes high above the set. Rain scenes always create a challenge for us; water and A/C electricity do not mix. We have to protect all of our lights, we have to put our cable connections up out of the water, and we have to use caution to not get electrocuted or electrocute anyone else on the set.

The second unit filmed the final exterior scenes where Tango and Cash drive through the compound of the bad guy (played by Jack Palance) blowing up everything in sight. We filmed these scenes in a quarry in Irwindale, California, at night, of course. The special effects guys spent weeks setting up all the explosions. They had several 500-gallon natural gas tanks spotted all over the place. So, on the first night of shooting, they had the gas company send out a truck to top off all their tanks. When we got ready to shoot, the gas company guy, who wanted to be able to watch, decided he would hide in one of the little shacks built on the set. The problem was that the shack he was hiding in was scheduled to be blown up during the shot. They started rolling and blowing up stuff when somebody spotted the guy in the shack. They shouted at him to get out of there, so he took off running as explosions were going off all around him. About 10 seconds after he got out, the shack he was in was blown to smithereens. As he ran through the set, he was seen on several of the cameras. Luckily, they had about a dozen cameras running, so they were able to edit him, and his gas company shirt, out. I am sure, when it was over, he had to change his linen!

During some of the scenes, the special effects guys were shooting rockets. Real rockets! They, of course, had no war heads or explosives, but they were real rockets. Most of the rockets ended up in the walls of the quarry, but a couple of times the rockets went just over the edge of the quarry and shot across the eight-lane freeway that ran next to the quarry. Imagine someone driving down that freeway in the middle of the night, next to a quarry in the middle of nowhere, as a rocket flies across their windshield. OMG!

NAVY SEALS (1989)

Starring:	Charlie Sheen, Michael Biehn, Joanne Whalley, Rick Rossovich, Cyril O'Rielly, Bill Paxton, Dennis Haysbert
Director:	Lewis Teague
Cinematographer:	John Alonzo
Lighting Gaffer:	Aggie Aguilar
Best Boy:	Paul Caven (screen credit)
Rigging Gaffer:	Kevin Lang

We filmed this movie from September through December of 1989. In September and October, we filmed in Virginia Beach, Norfolk, and Richmond, Virginia, as well as Washington D.C. In November and December, we filmed in Spain. Most of the filming in Spain was done in and around Cartagena and at an old Spanish Army barracks there and at an ancient Roman excavation site. We also filmed in Almeria, Málaga, Tarifa, Cadiz, and Madrid.

Aggie and I jumped at the prospect of doing this film. Two months in Spain, are you kidding me? Unfortunately, the show was ill-fated from the beginning. We had not worked with the cameraman before (I cannot remember his name) but, it did not really matter because he was fired after the first couple of weeks. The new cameraman was John Alonzo. I had worked with John a couple of times, on *Casey's Shadow* and *Cheap Detective,* (where I earned my John Alonzo white cap) but Aggie had never worked with him.

Not too far into the filming, Michael Biehn and Charlie Sheen started disagreeing with the director about how he was laying out scenes. Lewis Teague was alright, he had directed a few notable movies like *The Jewel of the Nile,* but he was primarily a TV director and he went back to directing TV movies after this filming experience. One of the scenes the actors objected to involved a scripted scene that had them playing volleyball. They said it was too much like a similar scene in *Top Gun*. So, Bill Paxton wrote a scene where they all play golf instead of volleyball and that was what we filmed. By the time we got to Spain, it was an out-and-out mutiny. This is the only movie I have ever worked on where the actors actually mutinied against the director. Michael and Charlie were not even talking to Lewis any more. They were laying out the scenes with John Alonzo while Lewis was relegated to sitting in his director's chair reduced to only saying "Action" and "Cut." The mutiny was not all of the actors; it was mostly Charlie and Michael.

Our Virginia Beach crew was great but, I was pleasantly surprised at the quality of the Spanish crew. Most of them were very experienced. Their key electrician, Casimiro Dengra Agusti, worked on many of the "spaghetti westerns" filmed in Spain. Most of the crew knew a little English and wanted to learn more hoping they could get hired on a crew in the upcoming Olympics in Barcelona, Spain. We had some challenges with the equipment in Spain. We rented all of our lighting equipment from a Mole-Richardson equipment rental house in Madrid. Mole-Richardson is an old Hollywood movie lighting equipment manufacturer founded in 1927. Every studio has mostly 'Mole' lights, they also rent their equipment. The main problem was everything in Spain is 220 volts AC and not all of their old Mole equipment was grounded properly. It was always a challenge to not get zapped. Kevin Lang had his own crew for rigging. He also had an interpreter with him. He did a lot of big rigs on this show. Kevin taught his crew how we wrap-up some of our larger cables. We wrap them in a large figure eight configuration so we can more easily pull the cable back out when we need it again. His crew would teasingly call him Señor Ocho, meaning Mr. Eight.

I would work with Joanne Walley on our next film, *Shattered*. Rick, Cyril and Bill were all great guys. Dennis Haysbert was especially caring. He was just a kind, gentle person, low key with a magnificent deep voice and a wonderfully broad, contagious smile. He would always say "Hi" to Denise and Danielle when they came on the set. Later Dennis landed a pretty good gig as the spokesperson for Allstate Insurance.

Denise and Danielle were able to join me in Virginia Beach and then came with me to Spain. They stayed in Spain for the first several weeks but we started working nights and traveling around Spain so

Denise decided to return home. I drove them to the airport, but because I had to get back to work before they left, I had to just drop them off. Denise told me later what had happened.

Because Danielle uses a wheelchair, Denise's first problem was getting them upstairs to the departure area. She realized she needed a key to operate the elevator. She finally found someone to open the elevator. Then, when they got to the check-in desk there seemed to be a problem with their tickets. The counter person decided to call security. An Army officer showed up with two guards armed with automatic rifles slung over their shoulders and said, "Follow me, Señora, por favor." He then took them into the office of the head of security.

The man sitting behind the desk was right out of Central Casting. He was wearing a pinstripe suit, he had jet black hair all slicked back, and a black pencil mustache. He said: "Give me your passports, por favor." Denise said, "I'll let you look at our passport but I will not give you our passports". That is when things got tense. He started to interrogate her, "Where are you from, what are you doing here, where are you going, is your daughter smuggling weapons in her wheelchair?" Finally, he asked, "What are you doing in Spain?" Denise said, "I'm here with my husband who is here making a movie." He then jumped up and said, "A movie?" as he started making the motion of cranking a camera in front of his face. She explained what movie it was and where we were shooting. Excited, he ran from behind the desk saying, "A movie with Charlie Sheen?" She said, "Yes." He then took her by the arm saying, "Come with me, Señora, por favor."

He took them up to the VIP lounge and asked if there was anything he could do for them. He got them both drinks and snacks and stayed with them until their flight was boarding. He then escorted them to the gate. He apparently was a big fan of American movies. When Denise told me what had happened, I was so sorry for what she had to go through all alone in a foreign country. But she is such a strong person. That is one of the things I really love about her. She was able to handle the situation and protect Danielle. She's the best!

Navy Seals – The Cast

Charlie Sheen's Good Wishes

Navy Seals – The Crew

Jon Alonso in his white cap

**Location: a Roman excavation site
in central Cartagena**

Full Spanish Crew

Spanish Shooting Crew

Virginia Beach Shooting Crew

And Now a Word from Our Sponsors

Between movies, Aggie and I would work on commercials. Commercials are a separate branch of the business. It is a pretty good gig if you can get hooked up with a couple of commercial producers. Some people do nothing but commercials their whole career. Commercial productions pay a lot more than any other productions, but they have smaller crews and most commercials only shoot 2 to 4 days, so you need to book as many as you can if you want to make a good living. Luckily, we were just filling in with commercials so when our next movie opportunity would come up, we were gone.

One of the problems with working commercials is that some of the commercial production companies are rather fly-by-night. We had to get to the bank as soon as we could to cash the check. Sometimes only about the first 20 people's checks were good, after that they ran out of money. On the other end of the spectrum, we worked on an Australian shampoo commercial. At the end of the day a guy shows up with a suitcase. The suitcase was full of U.S. dollars. You gave him an invoice and he gave you cash. Those were nice!

I worked on a lot of the McDonald's Ham-Burglar commercials, a lot of Jack-in-the-Box commercials, car commercials and beer commercials. We did a "Dr. Pepper" commercial in 1983 titled *The Hunchback* that won a CLIO award for best commercial. We filmed it on Universal Studio's back lot. It showed Quasimodo tied to the pillory. You hear him cry out softly, "Donna Pema." The people move in closer to hear what he is saying he repeats, "Donna Pema." When the people finally move close enough to hear him, they realize he was asking for a "Dr. Pepper."

I worked on a cat food commercial with "Morris the Cat." We filmed it way out in the middle of nowhere up in the Santa Susana Mountains north of Los Angeles. The scene was Morris sitting on a corral talking to a horse, of course, of course. Everything was going fine until the horse sneezed and spooked the cat. Morris took off running through the waist-high California chaparral. Every once-in-a-while, we would see a little bit of a cat's tail pop up over the thicket. The cat's trainer panicked. He was watching his million-dollar meal ticket running into the wilderness more than likely to become coyote finger food. They called lunch and we went to eat while they sent out a search party for Morris. They eventually found him and brought him back, but he was so dirty and full of stickers and brambles that we could not film him—so they called a wrap.

In July of 1986 we did a Merrill Lynch commercial called *Bulls Across America*, a take-off of the Hands Across America movement at the time. We filmed the Merrill Lynch bull in several scenic locations. We filmed in the California Redwood forests near Crescent City, and at the Grand Teton's in Jackson, Wyoming. On the first day of shooting, the director noticed that the black bull we were using was not totally black. It seemed he had some very noticeable white hairs on his penis. The director, of course, did not want that, so the lowest man on the bull wrangler's totem pole got the job of spraying the bull's penis with black color hair spray every day.

One of the wonderful things about this job is that we get to see many of the country's natural wonders. The weird part about this job is all the different places we eat lunch. I have a photo of us eating lunch among the giant redwood trees on this commercial. I wish I would have taken photos of all the unusual places we have eaten lunch; it would make for an interesting coffee table book. Most of the time we eat in people's back yards or church parking lots. One time we ate lunch next to a toxic waste pool at an oil refinery in Louisiana... Bon Appetit!

In December of 1986, we worked on a commercial at Disneyland for a new ride they were just opening. It was called "Star Tour"—a kind of a spaceship flight simulator. It would toss and turn and bump up and down like a rollercoaster or like we were flying through *Star Wars*. Just like the last rollercoaster I had to ride on in *The Entertainer,* the cameraman and the light guy had to be facing backwards with no seat belt. At least with this ride there was no chance of falling out a hundred feet in the air. We had to film this commercial at night when Disneyland was closed. It was really strange seeing Main Street, the castle and all of Disneyland dark with only work light on, but even stranger to see Mickey Mouse, Goofy and Snow White clocking-in in the morning as we were leaving.

We worked on a car commercial in Joshua Tree National Park. It was a reunion of sorts. The key grip, Tom Ramsey, had worked with Laszlo and Aggie on Easy Rider. We worked from sunrise to sunset. There was one shot where you see a vulture in the foreground as the car drives by. They wanted the vulture to spread its wings as the car went by. It took about twenty takes but we finally got it.

Joshua Tree is one of my favorite National Parks. There is nothing more inspiring than a sunrise or a sunset in Joshua Tree National Park. Joshua trees are some of the oldest species on earth and are one of the species predicted to be eliminated from Joshua Tree National Park, with ecological research suggesting a high probability that their populations will be reduced by 90% by the end of the 21st century.

In September of 1993 Aggie got a job with *America's Most Wanted*. It was scheduled to be a five day shoot. We had not worked for a while so a five-day shoot sounded good. We were supposed to expose a fugitive criminal. The only problem was, when we showed up for our first day of filming, we found out that the guy turned himself in the night before. So, he couldn't stay a fugitive for four more days and then turn himself in? So much for America's most wanted.

Joshua Tree

Aggie Aguilar & Tom Ramsey

Shooting in Joshua Tree with Vulture

Shooting In Joshua Tree

Shooting In Joshua Tree 2

Sunrise at Joshua Tree

Sunset at Joshua Tree

189

Shooting the Bull

Shooting the Bull in the Grand Tetons

Shooting the Bull in the Redwoods

Shooting in the Redwoods

Lunch in the Redwoods

The End of the Second Golden Age

By the late 1980s, early 1990s the Second Golden Age was waning. Many independent producers were no longer independent; they had aligned more and more with the studios again. The studios once again had more control over the product. They were no longer interested in the small, edgy, character driven, artsy films. They wanted the big budget, Harry Potter, Marvel Comics fantasy films with lots of computer-generated action. With the advent of more and more ancillary markets, video, Pay Per View, premium cable like HBO, Showtime, Cinemax, streaming services, cable television, network television and television syndication, it is hard to lose money on a movie these days. Not all films are released to theaters anymore. Many go straight to DVD or other ancillary markets.

That change in markets resulted in a change in focus (no pun intended). The producers' attitude became "If it is not going to be shown on a big screen, or if it is shot on video tape, then we do not need to worry that much about how it looks. If it is only going to be seen on a TV screen or on people's phones, why do we need to waste all this time on lighting?"

This shift resulted in the quality of lighting becoming less and less important. This was not true on all films; there were many fine films being made, but the overwhelming number of movies made spend more money on special effects and computer generation than lighting. I can only hope that the pendulum will eventually swing back the other way and we may have a Third Golden Age of Movies.

THE END OF AN ERA

SHATTERED (1990)

Starring:	Tom Berenger, Bob Hoskins, Greta Scacchi, Joanne Whalley, Corbin Bernsen
Director:	Wolfgang Petersen
Cinematographer:	Laszlo Kovacs
Lighting Gaffer:	Aggie Aguilar
Best Boy:	Paul Caven (screen credit)

We filmed this movie from January through June of 1990. We filmed on stage at Sony Studios (the old MGM Studios), in and around Los Angeles, in San Francisco and in Cannon Beach, Oregon.

The scenes at the Hacienda Hotel were at the former Gillette Mansion. I have filmed there many times on shows like *Frances* and other movies and commercials. King Camp Gillette was the inventor of the disposable razor. He is the founder of the Gillette razor brand. Gillette built this mansion in Malibu Canyon in 1928 and the property is now called King Gillette Ranch. Gillette willed the mansion to the Catholic Church upon his death in 1932, but the Church was unable to maintain the property so they sold it. It has changed hands many times over the years, being everything from a private residence to a school for female Japanese exchange students. The property has been open to the public since 2007.

The two houses in the film were both in Southern California. The beach house was in the Malibu area. In the movie, however, you see the Golden Gate Bridge in the background. This is done by a process called "matting." They would put a blank mat in the camera or in the shot to block out the area that they want to enhance. Later they insert footage, in this case footage of the Golden Gate Bridge, to fill in the blank spot. They often used mat shots years ago; today, it is all computer-generated. The scenes in the forest were filmed at the John Muir Woods National Monument north of San Francisco. The final scene, where the Mercedes goes over the cliff, was filmed at Cannon Beach, Oregon.

This is the only film we did with Wolfgang Petersen. He was a very enjoyable person, easy going, and a good director. He was best known for his multi award-winning film *Das Boot,* the riveting story of a German U-boat during the "Battle of the Atlantic" in World War II.

This film had a good cast. Tom Berenger was great, and Bob Hoskins was really friendly. It amazes me how he, as an actor, can put on a New York accent. He is English and normally speaks with a broad English accent. I think he did a fantastic job on this film. He had starred in many films, but he was probably best known for the film *Who Framed Roger Rabbit.* Greta Scacchi did a good job on this movie. She is Italian born and best known for her role in the movie *Presumed Innocent.* Nicole Kidman originally read for this part. Aggie and I had just worked with Joanne Whalley on *Navy Seals.* Corbin Bernsen was charming, but the character you see in films is, in reality, him.

PAUL CAVEN

KINDERGARTEN COP (1990)

Starring:	Arnold Schwarzenegger
Director:	Ivan Reitman
Cinematographer:	Michael Chapman
Lighting Gaffer:	Les Kovacs

After *Shattered* and the first *Radio Flyer,* but before the real *Radio Flyer,* (I will explain in a minute) I filled in on the crew of *Kindergarten Cop.* I was hired by the best boy, Benny McNulty, who had worked for Aggie and me on several shows. I only lasted a couple of weeks before I quit. I quit the show because I could not stand being in the same room with Arnold Schwarzenegger. In my opinion, he is an arrogant, loud, self-centered, womanizing, repulsive, person! I felt so bad for the script consultant on the show. She was an attractive, middle-aged, married woman; she was very professional and an excellent script supervisor. I had worked with her before on *Electric Horseman* and worked with her later on *Sleepwalker.*

Because of Schwarzenegger's poor performance, the script consultant had to approach him after almost every shot to tell him what lines he missed or something else he might have done wrong. Every time she would get close to him, he would try to grope her right there on the set. She, of course, tried to stop him and did her best to protect her dignity, but he was the STAR, so neither she, nor anyone else was able to stop him. This behavior, of course, was repeated with just about every female on the set. It was like he thought they all were there for him to play with. I think he is a disgusting human being!

RADIO FLYER (1990)

Starring:	Lorraine Bracco, Adam Baldwin, John Heard, Elijah Wood, Joseph Mazzello, Ben Johnson, Tom Hanks
Director:	Richard Donner
Cinematographer:	Laszlo Kovacs
Lighting Gaffer:	Aggie Aguilar
Best Boy:	Paul Caven *(*screen credit)

In June of 1990, I received a call from Jerry Boatright, the gaffer I worked with on *An Innocent Man* and *Tango and Cash.* He was starting a new movie called *Radio Flyer,* and he wanted me to work as a lamp operator. It was to be directed by the film's screen writer, David Evans. As I have said more than once, writers do not make good directors. He was no exception.

This film was originally cast with Rosanna Arquette and two other child actors. After eleven days of shooting, all the suits (including producer Michael Douglas) showed up on the set and pulled the plug. They did not like what they were seeing in the dailies. They decided to not only change the director, but also to change the actors and the crew. They would recast and restart the production with a brand-new crew. They purposely did not rehire anyone who was on the first production.

In late September, I received a call from Aggie saying that Laszlo was starting a new movie called *Radio Flyer,* and I, of course, would be best boy. It would be directed by our good friend Richard Donner, who we worked with on *The Toy,* and he wanted us for his crew. I do not think they ever realized that I worked on the original show as a lamp operator, because now I was hired as best boy. The only other person re-hired from the first production was Larry Madrid and his German Shepherd, Burt.

We filmed in Los Angeles, Sonora, and Novato, California, from October 1990 to February 1991. The house in Novato was in the former Hamilton Air Force Base housing, which is apparent in the uniformity of all the houses in those neighborhood scenes.

The merry-go-round scene was filmed at the merry-go-round in Griffith Park in Los Angeles. The producers told the crew that we could bring our families in to work in the merry-go-round scene, so Denise and Danielle came to the set to be in the movie. The second assistant director placed them on a bench to the side of the merry-go-round. When Dick Donner came to set up the scene, he saw Denise and Danielle sitting on the side. He said, "Hi Denise, how come you're sitting over there?" Denise said they had placed them there. Dick said to the second assistant director, "No, put Danielle up on the merry-go-round." Danielle was not in the movie, but it did not matter to her; she just enjoyed being on the merry-go-round and not sitting on the side watching the other kids on the merry-go-round. Dick Donner knew that was what she wanted. It was such a warm, insightful, act of kindness that demonstrated his sensitivity and compassion. A few weeks later, Danielle had to have surgery on her legs and Dick sent her flowers and a teddy bear. He is a marvelous person.

This movie did not do well at the box office. I think most people did not understand it or did not get the symbolism. Some people did not like the ending. It is not really clear what is reality and what is childhood fantasy. It is a very moving film about child abuse. The movie is about the innocence of childhood, the grandness of being naive and imaginative, all being ripped apart by an abusive stepfather.

I think Dick Donner did an inspired job of filming the abusive stepfather (Adam Baldwin) in a sinister manner from the child's point of view. You never get a good look at him. He is seen mostly from below the waist or in silhouette. John Heard played the Sheriff. We had worked with him before on *Heartbeat*. The two boys (Elijah Wood and Joseph Mazzello) did an excellent job. Elijah, of course, went on later to star in *The Lord of the Rings* series. Joseph also went on to have a good career being in such movies as *Jurassic Park* and *River Wild*. It was a real joy to work with Ben Johnson, a veteran of many western movies and a real cowboy. Tom Hanks narrates the film and had a small but important on-screen part as the adult Mike, the Elijah Wood character. Aggie had a small part in this film also as the junk yard owner.

Radio Flyer – The Crew

The Whole Radio Flyer Crew (Photo Credit: Unknown)

SLEEPWALKERS (1991)

Starring:	Brian Krause, Mädchen Amick, Alice Krige
Director:	Mick Garris
Screenplay:	Stephen King
Cinematographer:	Rodney Charters
Lighting Gaffer:	Aggie Aguilar
Best Boy:	Paul Caven *(*screen credit)

This was my one and only "horror movie." It was written by Stephen King. I have never been a big Stephen King fan, so when I started reading this script, I kept saying to myself, "I can't read any more of this junk. They're ripping off people's hands, stabbing a guy to death with a corn cob, ramming a pencil in a guy's ear, and mutilating cats." The other problem I had with the script was the incestuous relationship between the mother sleepwalker Alice Krige and her son Brian Krause. I never finished reading the script. I wish I had never done the movie.

Stephen King had a cameo part in the film as the cemetery caretaker. Seeing him on the set, I thought he was a very strange person. They also had cameos from several other horror movie writers and directors. Tobe Hooper: *The Texas Chain Saw Massacre*, Clive Barker: *Hell Raiser* (series), Joe Dante: *The Howling,* and John Landis: *An American Werewolf in London.*

We filmed this movie in and around Los Angeles from June through August 1991. The house that the sleepwalkers lived in was on the Warner Brothers back lot and was originally the *Walton's* home. I guess we destroyed the karma of that building; I could only imagine: "Goodnight John-boy, I think I'll rip your head off! Sleep tight!"

This was our only show with cameraman Rodney Charters. I was not impressed; he is no Laszlo Kovacs or Sven Nykvist, although he was foreign, from Canada. I have nothing against Canadians, some of my best friends are Canadian, but I thought he was kind of a jerk. He kept telling us how fantastic his Canadian crew was; I know there are some great people working in Canada, and they do good work, but I did not want to hear how much better his Canadian crew was compared to my crew.

The film had a pretty good cast. Brian Krause was in his early twenties and really friendly. He would hang out with the lighting crew in our equipment truck after work and have a beer with us. He later ended up being a regular on the TV series *Charmed.* Alice Krige was very pleasant. Mädchen Amick was also very nice. Her first name is a German word meaning a girl. The actors who played the parents of Mädchen Amick, Cindy Pickett and Lyman Ward, were the same couple who played the mom and dad in *Ferris Bueller's Day Off* and are married to each other in real life.

Sleepwalkers – The Cast and Crew

Cast and Crew
(Photo by Sam Emmerson)

200

CHAPLIN (1991)

Starring:	Robert Downey Jr., Geraldine Chaplin, Paul Rhys, Moira Kelly, Anthony Hopkins, Dan Aykroyd, Kevin Kline, Marisa Tomei, James Woods
Director:	Sir Richard Attenborough
Cinematographer:	Sven Nykvist
Lighting Gaffer:	Aggie Aguilar
Best Boy:	Paul Caven (screen credit)

The beginning of this movie was filmed in England and Switzerland. Aggie and I did not work on that part of the film. We filmed the rest of the film in and around the Los Angeles area from October through December of 1991. The working title was *Charlie,* but the makers of the 1968 Cliff Robertson movie *Charly* complained that the title would lead to confusion with their movie, so the film was renamed *Chaplin.*

The movie was released 15 years to the day of Charlie Chaplin's death. We filmed all the exterior scenes of the Mack Sennet studios and the Chaplin studios in Fillmore, California. They picked Fillmore because it looks like what Hollywood looked like in the early days. The original Chaplin Studio is still in Hollywood on La Brea Blvd. It is now the home of A&M Records and the original movie sound stages are still there.

Robert Downing Jr. did a phenomenal job on this film which was incredible considering, as we found out later, he was a "functioning" heroin addict at the time. Thank God he turned his life around and is now one of Hollywood's top male actors. His portrayal of Charlie Chaplin was spot on. He had studied all of Chaplin's films and had his mannerisms down pat. He was nominated for both an Academy Award and a Golden Globe.

The film was nominated or won several other prestigious awards for acting, director, art director, make up, music, costume design, as well as cinematography. Geraldine Chaplin was also nominated for a

201

Golden Globe Award. She is Charlie Chaplin's daughter with his last wife Oona. Oona was the daughter of the playwright Eugene O'Neill. Chaplin and Oona were married from 1943 until his death in 1977.

Geraldine plays Chaplin's mother in the film, her real-life grandmother, who went insane and who Charlie had to place in an institution while he was still a young boy. Geraldine is known for her dramatic roles, as opposed to her father, and this was a dramatic role. She did an extraordinary job. Moira Kelly plays Oona Chaplin. Moira is an accomplished actress and has performed in many films, but she is probably best known as the voice of "Nala" in the *Lion King* animated series.

I was disappointed that we did not get to work with Anthony Hopkins. All of his scenes were filmed in Switzerland. His character is the only principal character in the entire film that is fictional. He plays a writer who is working on Chaplin's biography, which is, of course, the vehicle used to tell Chaplin's life story. Richard Attenborough has cast Anthony Hopkins in almost every film he has directed.

I was also a little disappointed working with Dan Aykroyd. He was not as friendly as one might think. He kept to himself and only came on the set to shoot his scenes and then went back to his trailer. Of course, sometimes people who are entertainers, not actors, by trade, e.g. comedians, have to work a little harder at being an actor than most. Also, some actors, particularly "method actors," need to block everything out to stay in character and do not relate to anything else in the real world. Method actors, by definition, are self-centered; it is all about them and their character.

Sir Richard Attenborough was a great guy; I mean a GREAT guy! He was a talented actor in such classic films as *The Great Escape* and *A Bridge Too Far,* which he also directed. In addition, he directed the memorable films *Gandhi* and *A Chorus Line.* He was knighted by Queen Elizabeth II in 1976. On the set, all of his minions were required to call him "Sir Richard," but he wanted the crew to call him by his nickname, "Dickie." He loved the crew, and I think deep down he thought of himself as being on the crew. Sometimes I thought he would rather be a crew member than a director or an actor. One day, one of my guys became ill and had to be taken to the hospital. That night, after a long day's work, Dickie took the time to call the hospital and talk to my electrician to see how he was doing.

That tells you more about the man than any film he has ever done. He was genuinely concerned.

This was our third film with Sven Nykvist. Aggie and I would do one more film with Sven. He was a warm sensitive artiste who used light like an artist would use a brush to create a masterpiece, and this was a masterpiece. I loved Sven; he was a quiet, soft spoken, delightful human being.

During the scene when Chaplin is at work on the movie *Shoulder Arms,* at the end of the day, he asks his long-time cameraman, Roland Totheroh, the running question, "How's the light, Rollie?" and the rest of the crew replies "Better down at Barney's bar." This was the cue for production to end for the day - the "light" Chaplin was referring to was the lite beer served at Barney Oldfield's bar, which was the favorite drinking and hangout spot for the crew after filming. Things have not changed much since then.

Totheroh and Chaplin had a working relationship that was to last 37 years from 1915 until Chaplin was exiled from the United States in 1952. They met while Rollie, who was from San Francisco, was working with the Essanay Company in Niles, California (later to be incorporated with Fremont in northern California). He was working as an actor/cameraman on westerns with Gilbert M. 'Broncho Billy' Anderson, who acted and directed over 500 westerns in the early 1900s. Chaplin also filmed several of his movies in Niles.

HOME ALONE 2: LOST IN NEW YORK (1992)

Starring: Macaulay Culkin, Joe Pesci, Daniel Stern, Catherine O'Hara, John Heard

Director: Chris Columbus

Cinematographer: Julio Macat

Lighting Gaffer: Colin Campbell

Best Boy: Paul Caven (screen credit)

The majority of this filming took place in New York and Chicago. I only worked on the part they filmed in Los Angeles in April and May of 1992. The gaffer, Colin Campbell, had worked for me and Aggie as an electrician 20 years earlier, so when he needed a best boy for the Los Angeles shoot, he called me. Everything we filmed was on the Universal Studio lot. The renovated house where Kevin sets up his traps is not actually in New York City. All the scenes of the exterior of the house and the surrounding neighborhood were filmed at Universal Studios backlot on Brownstone Street. We also filmed some of the interiors on stage.

Macaulay Culkin was paid 8 million dollars to star in this movie, the biggest paycheck ever to a 12-year-old child. From my perspective, Macaulay was one of those child actors who had a lot more money than sense, and his parents did not help any. He had all kinds of legal problems with his parents because of the money. He dropped out of the business in 1994 after doing *Richie Rich* and did not work for almost a decade. He did a few bit parts after that but he never had a comeback.

Joe Pesci and Daniel Stern were a kick to work with. They were always laughing and joking around on the set. I had worked with John Heard before on *Heartbeat* and *Radio Flyer* and would work with him again on *My Fellow Americans*.

Donald Trump makes an appearance in this film in the lobby of the Plaza Hotel where Kevin asks him for directions. Donald Trump owned the hotel during the making of this film. He bought it from

The Childs Company (now called Sonesta) for $407.5 million, and sold it later to Troy Richard Campbell for $325 million for a loss of $82.5 million, not exactly an "Artful Deal." (Source: IDMb Trivia Section of Home Alone 2.)

The premier screening for the show was at a theater in Century City. They had a carnival set up for the kids and all kinds of games. When it came time for the screening, we got to walk down the red carpet with all the cameras flashing.

Home Alone 2: Lost in New York – The Crew

Full Crew
(Photo Credit: Melinda Sue Gordon)

Lighting Crew
Colin Cambell (center back) (left to right) Paul Caven, Darryl Herzon,
Louis Ramos, Rudy Munoz, Bruce Schultz, Adam Glick

SLEEPLESS IN SEATTLE (1992)

Starring:	Tom Hanks, Meg Ryan, Ross Malinger, Bill Pullman, David Hyde Pierce, Rosie O'Donnell, Rob Reiner, Rita Wilson, Victor Garber
Director:	Nora Ephron
Cinematographer:	Sven Nykvist
Chief Lighting Technician:	Aggie Aguilar
Best Boy:	Paul Caven (screen credit official title Assistant Chief Lighting Technician)

We filmed the majority of this movie in Seattle, Washington, from July to October of 1992. We filmed for 10 weeks in Seattle, 3 days in Chicago, 6 days in Baltimore, then 2 weeks in New York. I did not do the New York shoot. The interior sets of the houseboat in Seattle, the interiors of Meg's apartment in Baltimore, as well as the last scenes, and the night exteriors of the Empire State Building Observation Deck were all filmed on a make shift stage in Seattle. The interior of the airplane scenes were filmed at the Boeing plant in Renton, Washington, inside the sales mock-up for their brand-new Boeing 747.

The first day of shooting was on stage in the houseboat set with Tom and the boy. After seeing the dailies, Nora decided she was unhappy with the performance of the little boy she cast, so we filmed around the boy for a couple of days while she recast the part. She ended up casting Ross Malinger. I think Ross did a marvelous job for only being 8 years old. Meg Ryan and Tom Hanks only share approximately two minutes of screen time together. Both Tom and Meg were ok to work with. They were not overly friendly to the crew, but they were cordial.

David Hyde Pierce had a small part in this film. At that time, David was not very well known. He had only worked on a dozen or so movies and TV shows where he was credited as David Pierce. He changed his screen credit to David Hyde Pierce on this film and immediately got a major role that lasted for over ten years on the TV show *Frasier*. It is all in the name! He plays Meg's brother who works at the George Peabody Library in Baltimore. The Peabody Library is an enormous building built in 1878. As one enters into a large open center area, looking up one sees six stories full of 300,000 books. It has been described as a Cathedral of Books. That was the most books I have ever seen all at one time. Rob Reiner was cool to work with; he was raised in the industry by his father Carl Reiner and was very at ease on the set and with the crew. Rosie O'Donnell... not so much. She never even acknowledged the crew.

Nora Ephron was a very pleasant person, but she could be somewhat indecisive and obsessive at times. The casting of the boy was a perfect example. She cast the first boy and then changed her mind after the first day of shooting. She would obsess about Meg's costume or hair, going back and forth on what she liked while the whole crew stood around waiting for her to line up the next scene. Remember my theory that writers do not make good directors? Nora was a very perceptive, insightful, sensitive writer. She wrote this screenplay, but, she had only directed one other movie before this show. She was good at directing the actors, but she was not very good technically. She relied on Sven a great deal.

This was my last film with Sven. I just loved working for Sven. He and Aggie would work together again on *Mixed Nuts* (with Nora Ephron), but I was working on another movie when they started it, so I could not work on that show except for a couple of weeks of rigging Christmas lights on the Venice Boardwalk toward the end of the show.

Sleepless In Seattle – The Crew

Crew Photo
(Photo Credit: Bruce McBroom)

Seattle Crew

THE NEXT KARATE KID (1993)

Starring:	Pat Morita, Hilary Swank, Michael Ironside, Chris Conrad
Director:	Christopher Cain
Producer:	Jerry Weintraub
Cinematographer:	Laszlo Kovacs
Chief Lighting Technician:	Aggie Aguilar
Assistant Chief Lighting Technician:	Paul Caven (screen credit)

We filmed this movie from June through August of 1993 mostly in and around Boston, except the opening scenes, which we filmed at Fort Myer, Virginia, and Arlington National Cemetery. The exteriors and interiors of the high school were filmed in Brookline, Mass.; the house was in Newton, Mass.; and we filmed the Prom scenes in the gym at Tufts University.

Pat Morita was a joy to work with. He was friendly and always had time for his fans. Hilary, who turned 19 years old on this show, was very sociable also. She had worked on several TV shows, but this was her first starring movie role. The producers were not really happy with her performance at first, so they hired an acting coach for her. It apparently worked because this would be a breakout role for her. She would go on later to win two Academy Awards, a Golden Globe, and several other awards for her work on *Boys Don't Cry,* and *Million Dollar Baby.*

The culminating scene of the movie was when Pat and Hilary go to a deserted rock quarry to release the hawk that she had been nursing back to health. The problem was that when we filmed the release of the bird into the wild, you can see in the movie that the hawk was being harassed by a little bird that obviously had a nest nearby. The hawk's trainer could not get the hawk to come back because the little bird kept chasing him off. He finally got the hawk back, but he could not get him to fly very far for take two. We were only able to shoot it once.

We were on location for the 4th of July, so the producer, Jerry Weintraub, arranged a party at his home in Kennebunkport, Maine. He rented party buses to take us up there from Boston and we had a momentous 4th of July party. He also invited his old friends Mr. and Mrs. George H. W. Bush. It was a thrill to talk to and shake hands with an ex-President of the United States, even for this old dyed-in-the-wool Democrat.

The Next Karate Kid – The Cast and Crew

Pat Morita's Good Wishes

Gen. Colin Powell & Jerry Weintraub

Former President George H.W. Bush

Former First Lady Barbara Bush

JUNIOR (1994)

Starring:	Arnold Schwarzenegger, Danny DeVito, Emma Thompson
Director:	Ivan Reitman
Cinematographer:	Adam Greenberg
Chief Lighting Technician:	Steve McGee

My old friend Kevin Lang was the best boy on this show and he hired me to fill in for a couple of weeks while I was between jobs. Kevin worked with Aggie and me on a number of films. As a matter of fact, we brought him with us to Spain as a rigging gaffer on *Navy Seals*. They filmed the majority of this movie in the San Francisco area, but I only worked on the Los Angeles filming in April 1994.

We filmed on stage at Universal Studios, on location at LAX airport, and the famous Biltmore Hotel in downtown Los Angeles. I cannot even estimate how many times I have filmed at the Biltmore Hotel. This was my first film with Kevin's new gaffer Steve McGee. Steve was a good guy, and I think he liked my work. I would later work with him and Kevin on *Sphere,* and they would hire me again for a few days on *What Lies Beneath.* This was also my first film with Adam Greenberg. I would work with him again also on *Sphere* (although I never worked on the shooting crew) and *Rush Hour.* He was never one of my favorite cameramen. I will talk more about him later. He, Ivan Reitman, and Arnold deserve each other. Danny De Vito was fun to work with. He joked around with the crew and everybody loved it.

What I did not know when I took the job was that the star of this show was Arnold Schwarzenegger. I probably would not have taken the job if I had known that, but it was only for a few weeks so I stayed. I mentioned before how much I disliked Arnold Schwarzenegger while working on *Kindergarten Cop.* He had a new annoying habit on this show; in addition to his usual de-humanizing womanizing and narcissistic personality disorder, he was now an avid cigar smoker.

By that time in the industry, smoking was not allowed on

shooting stages anymore. This, however, did not apply to Arnold as far as he was concerned. He would come strolling on the set puffing away on his smelly cigar. He would then start passing cigars out to all his minions, and they would all sit around the set puffing away, polluting our air. No one in the entire production had the guts to tell him no. Some other members of the crew and I would walk off stage whenever he would pull this inconsiderate, selfish and illegal stunt.

I had worked with Ivan Reitman on *Legal Eagles* and briefly on *Kindergarten Cop.* He was not a very pleasant person. He did not associate with the crew at all.

FREE WILLY 2: THE ADVENTURE HOME (1994)

Starring:	Jason James Richter, Francis Capra, Michael Madson, Jayne Atkinson, Mary Kate Schellhardt, August Shellenberg
Director:	Dwight Little
Cinematographer:	Laszlo Kovacs
Chief Lighting Technician:	Aggie Aguilar
Assistant Chief Lighting Technician:	Paul Caven (screen credit)

We filmed this movie from May through August of 1994. We filmed a little of it on stage at Warner Brothers, for a week in Astoria, Oregon, and for another week in Escondido, California, where we filmed the underwater scenes in a huge water tank. The majority of this film, however, was filmed on the San Juan Islands off the coast of Washington State.

We stayed at Friday Harbor on San Juan Island, but we shot most of the film on a small island that was an hour and a half boat ride to and from every day. It was great. We could get an extra hour or so of sleep in the morning, and on the ride home, they would stock a couple of coolers full of beer and cold drinks. It don't get no better than that! The cast was very enjoyable, particularly Michael Madson, who would hang out with the guys.

It was mind-blowing to watch the special effects guys work the animatronic whales. All of the footage of the actors with the whales was done with the animatronic whales. The whales were controlled from a large barge with a crane on it, to be able to lift the whales in and out of the water. They had a whole lot of cables coming out of the whales that controlled all the movements. They looked very real.

Free Willy 2: The Adventure Home – The Crew

Dutch Van Woert & Rudy Munoz

**Dutch Van Woert, Frank Jimenez, &
John Haselbusch**

**The crew doing an Iwo Jima
Left top to bottom: Aggie Aguilar,
John Haselbusch, Kim Kono
Right top to bottom: Ron Newburn,
Dutch Van Woert, Rudy Munoz**

Kim Kono & Paul Caven
(Photo credit: Rudy Munoz)

216

Free Willy 2: The Adventure Home – Filming On Location

Filming Willy

Filming Three Whales

Animatronic Willy

Riding Willy

Filming on the Barge

**Paul Caven –
Filming on the Barge**
(Photo Credit: Rudy Munoz)

COPYCAT (1994)

Starring:	Sigourney Weaver, Holly Hunter, Dermot Mulroney, William McNamara, Harry Connick Jr., J.E. Freeman
Director:	Jon Amiel
Cinematographer:	Laszlo Kovacs
Chief Lighting Technician:	Aggie Aguilar
Assistant Chief Lighting Technician:	Paul Caven (screen credit)

We filmed this movie in and around San Francisco from September through December of 1994. The stage work was done in a warehouse on the Naval Base on Treasure Island.

This film had an excellent cast. Sigourney Weaver was super. Whenever Denise and Danielle would visit the set, she would come over and make a point of saying hi to Danielle. I had worked with Holly Hunter a decade before on *Swing Shift*. Dermot Mulroney was very friendly also; a terrific guy. I had worked with him before on *Sunset* and would work with him again on another show. Harry Connick Jr. I think, did an exceptionally brilliant job with his character. Most entertainers, particularly singers, are usually cast as themselves or a character closely resembling themselves. This was definitely the exception to that rule. In this movie, Harry convincingly plays a psychopathic killer. His performance is chilling!

The final bathroom scene took eight days to shoot. In this reenactment scene, Sigourney Weaver actually spat in William McNamara's face without his prior knowledge. The reaction of anger and shock in his face is quite real. Sigourney's stunt girl got a broken nose filming the part of the scene where she gets wrestled to the ground by William McNamara.

Copycat – The Crew

COPYCAT '94

Full Crew
(Photo Credit: Ben Glass)

PAUL CAVEN

FATHER OF THE BRIDE Part II (1995)

Starring:	Steve Martin, Diane Keaton, Martin Short, Kimberly Williams, George Newbern, Kieran Culkin
Director:	Charles Shyler
Cinematographer:	William Fraker
Chief Lighting Technician:	Doug Pentek

We filmed this movie from January through March of 1995; most of it was filmed in the Pasadena area and at the CBS Studios in Studio City, California. I was just an extra electrician and worked on both the rigging and the shooting crews. I knew the gaffer, Doug Pentek, but had never worked with him before. I had worked with Bill Fraker before, but this would be my last film with Fraker. He was one of a kind, a true classic independent film maker. He retired a few years after this movie and passed away in 2010. I really liked Fraker. He just enjoyed making movies... a man after my own heart!

This show was a sequel to a remake. It was a sequel to *Father of the Bride I* (1991) which was a remake of the 1950 original with Spencer Tracy, Joan Bennett and Elizabeth Taylor. The actors were all fantastic. They had all worked together before on the original remake. Steve Martin was ok, but (like Dan Aykroyd) not overly friendly with the crew. He was nominated for a Golden Globe Award and an American Comedy Award for his work on this film. I had worked with Diane Keaton before on *Harry and Walter Go to New York,* and would work with her one more time before I retired. Martin Short was a kick to work with. He is one of those entertainers who is always "ON."

Kimberly Williams was lovely, and apparently country singer Brad Paisley felt the same. When the movie opened, aspiring country singer Brad Paisley went to see it in the local theater with hopes of running into an ex-girlfriend he had taken to see the first *Father of the Bride* remake. The ex did not show, but as he told an Atlanta radio

220

station later, he sat in the theater watching the lead actress and thought to himself, "I could marry a girl like her." A few years later, he not only married a girl like her, he married that particular girl - actress Kimberly Williams-Paisley. I had heard this story before in the industry, but the details I share here came from IMDb.com under Father of the Bride II in the Trivia section.

Kieran Culkin is the younger brother of Macaulay Culkin. I have mentioned before about life at the Culkin household, but Kieran was once quoted as saying, "Until my brother Mac started making major money, our house was really wild. The outside world didn't know how chaotic our life was because though we'd live at home like a bunch of little critters, we'd go off to school and act all sedate and normal. Trust me, there is no such thing as normal for a Culkin. I certainly had a better, less hectic life than Mac. He took all the pressure at home and on movie sets. My dad basically left me alone because I wasn't making enough money to warrant his scrutiny." (Source: IMDb.com, Father of the Bride, Kieran Culkin's bio/personal quotes.) My thought: Daddy Dearest!!!

PRIMAL FEAR (1995)

Starring:	Richard Gere, Laura Linney, John Mahoney, Frances McDormand, Edward Norton
Director:	Gregory Hoblit
Cinematographer:	Michael Chapman
Chief Lighting Technician:	Jono Kouzouyan
Lighting Technician:	Paul (Bones) Caven (screen credit)

We filmed this movie from May through July of 1995 at Paramount Studios as well as in several Los Angeles locations including filming at the Queen Mary (a location I have filmed at so many times I lost count). We also filmed a few days in Chicago and in Keystone, West Virginia. The footage we filmed in West Virginia was cut from the final movie. The original rough cut of the film detailed Aaron's small-town country life in West Virginia and discussions with his former junior high school teacher. The scenes were cut partly for running time and partly to avoid the producers tipping their hand and alerting the audience to the ultimate ending.

The story is about a young homeless street kid named Aaron, played by Edward Norton, who is taken in by the Archbishop of Chicago. When the Archbishop was found murdered, Aaron was the main suspect. A hot shot lawyer named Martin Vail, played by Richard Gere, takes on the case pro bono. Aaron is shy and speaks with a stammer. Vail is convinced Aaron is innocent. He later discovers a video of Aaron taken during a psychology exam that reveals another personality named Roy who is very aggressive and possibly able to have committed the crime.

This movie was Edward Norton's first movie. 2,100 actors read for the part of Aaron, including Leonardo DiCaprio. It was hard to understand why the producers would hire an unproven actor for such a deep, dark, difficult character. Edward did an impressive job with this character. He won, or was nominated for, 14 different awards, including being nominated for the Academy Award and winning a Golden Globe Award. His performance was extraordinary. It was Edward Norton's idea to stutter as Aaron, as it appeared nowhere in the original book or script. In addition, when "Roy" shoves Vail (Richard Gere) against the prison cell wall, Gere's shocked reaction is genuine, as that was another Norton ad-lib. Yet another Norton ad-lib is Roy's slow clap at the end when Vail realized what had happened. It is a very chilling ending.

The ending was running over 6 pages long, and the writers realized that would take far too much screen time. Richard Gere and Edward Norton began to improvise, and encouraged by the director and writer, pared the scene down to less than 2 pages with a much crisper ending.

I was hired on this film by my good friend Dutch Van Woert, who was the best boy. Dutch had worked with Aggie and me on several shows. He was one of our regular crew members. One of the other crew members was my friend Greg Kittelson, whose nickname was "Bones." Somehow, when they were doing the screen credits, someone decided to attach that nick name to my name, so my screen credit reads Paul (Bones) Caven, thanks Bones.

I knew the gaffer, Jono Kouzouyan, but had never worked for him. I had worked with Michael Chapman, who they called Chappie, before on the Arnold Schwarzenegger movie that I quit, *Kindergarten Cop.* Chappie had done such iconic movies as, *The Last Detail, Taxi Driver,* and *Raging Bull.* He was an easy-going, funny guy with a great sense of humor. He died in 2020 at the age of 84. He was one of the good guys.

I had worked with Richard Gere in 1975 on *Baby Blue Marine.* It was one of his first movies, and he had a small but pivotal part. Richard was a very kind, giving person and he is an activist for humanitarian causes.

Primal Fear – The Cast and Crew

Richard Gere's Good Wishes

The Cast and Crew
(Photo Credit: Ron Phillips)

MULTIPLICITY (1995)

Starring:	Michael Keaton, Andie MacDowell
Director:	Harold Ramis
Cinematographer:	Laszlo Kovacs
Chief Lighting Technician:	Aggie Aguilar
Assistant Chief Lighting Technician:	Paul Caven (screen credit)

We filmed this movie from August 1995 through January 1996. We filmed in the Los Angeles area including the Queen Mary (again), the still-under-construction Skirball Cultural Center, the Los Angeles Forum, and, the by-then closed, world famous Chasen's Restaurant, which at one time was a Hollywood hangout, the place to be and be seen.

The main housing construction site we filmed was a construction site in Pacific Palisades. We had to go back two or three times to shoot it at different stages of construction. Comically, its name in the script was "Vista de Nada," which translates to "View of Nothing." The interiors were filmed at Sony Studios. Their house exterior and interiors were all on stage.

This film was unique because of the fact that Michael Keaton plays four separate characters. Anytime more than one of those characters was in the scene, we would shoot Michael playing to a person in a head to toe green body suit. Then we would go back and shoot the exact same thing with Michael playing the other character with the green guy now playing the opposite character. It became even more complicated when we had all four Michael Keaton characters. Later, during editing, the green guy would be replaced by what was filmed with Michael Keaton. Nowadays, this would be done by computer generation, but back then they used the innovative green Chroma-color technology where the green guy can be replaced visually. This is the same technology used today for TV weather persons. They are standing in front of a green screen wall where their weather maps are shown. When broadcasting, the camera just shows a weather map where the green screen is.

So, if all four characters were in the scene, we would have to shoot that same scene four separate times with three green guys and Michael Keaton alternating with each character. The problem was that once you shoot the first film of the scene, absolutely nothing can change or be moved while Michael changed costumes and make-up to play the other parts. Once we got the first scene filmed, we had nothing to do. We could not change anything.

We should have known what was coming when, on the first day of shooting, they gave the crew yo-yos to play with, knowing that we would have a lot of time to kill. They also set aside a large portion of the stage and brought in a ping-pong table, a golf putting green and driving tee, weights, a basketball hoop, and a pool table. Towards the end of filming, we had a crew Olympics competition. We set up teams and competed on all the equipment. Another thing we did on this show was to have a "career day." We put everyone's name in one hat and all the on-set jobs in another hat. The director pulled the names out of the hat then pulled the job that that person would do out of the other hat. I got on the camera crew. Michael Keaton was a laborer. After everyone was assigned to their jobs, we rolled the camera and filmed a scene showing Michael Keaton sweeping the floor. That scene was never in the movie, of course, but we all had fun.

Michael Keaton was fun to work with. This was a very difficult role. He had to create four very different and unique characters, and he nailed it. Andie MacDowell did a good job with her character as well. It was not the meatiest role ever for her, after all this movie was all about the four Michael Keaton characters. But I think she did the best that could be done under the circumstances.

Ann Cusack had a part in this movie too. I have worked with three of the Cusack siblings. I worked with John on *Say Anything,* and later on *Midnight in the Garden of Good and Evil.* I would work with Joan on my next movie *My Fellow Americans,* as well as *Midnight in the Garden of Good and Evil,* and later on an episode of *Six Feet Under.* Even though I worked with Ann the most, Joan was my favorite Cusack. She was very friendly and outgoing with the crew, a real character. She would just hang out with the crew, and she knew everyone's name. She too had a part in *Say Anything,* plus I worked with her on a show I just filled in on called *My Blue Heaven.*

MY FELLOW AMERICANS (1996)

Starring:	Jack Lemmon, James Garner, Dan Aykroyd, John Heard, Wilford Brimley, Lauren Bacall, Bradley Whitford
Director:	Peter Segal
Cinematographer:	Julio Macat
Chief Lighting Technician:	Aggie Aguilar
Assistant Chief Lighting Technician:	Paul Caven (screen credit)

We filmed this movie from March through May 1996 in and around Los Angeles, as well as on stage at Warner Brothers, Washington D.C., and in and around Asheville, North Carolina. We filmed at the Biltmore Hotel in downtown Los Angeles and on the grounds of the Biltmore Estate in North Carolina.

This show had an all-star cast. I had worked with Jack Lemmon once before on the TV Movie *The Entertainer.* It was wonderful working with him again. He was a fantastic actor and a very enjoyable person. I had worked with Jim Garner twice before, first on his TV series *Nichols,* then on the movie *Sunset.* He was another one who liked the crew. Lauren Bacall had a small part in this show as Jack Lemmon's wife. She was pleasant but a little more aloof than Jack or Jim. This was my second film with Dan Aykroyd, and he did not do anything to change my opinion of him. For being a comedian, he is not very personable off screen. This was my fourth show with John Heard. I worked with him on *Heart Beat, Radio Flyer,* and *Home Alone 2.* I had worked with Wilford Brimley once before on *The Electric Horseman.* Conchata Ferrell had a small part in this film too. I had worked with her on the TV movie *Before and After.*

This movie could have been a really good movie but for some reason, the producers hired a rookie to direct it. Pete Segal was fresh out of USC Film School and primarily a TV director. He was nice

227

enough, but he really did not know what to do with the talent he had. Directing a TV show is a snap, there is a basic formula of required shots consisting of a wide shot (a master shot showing basically the geography of the room), medium shots (shots showing groups of two or three), and then close-ups. Pete's problem was that he did not know how to think outside the box for movies.

I had worked with this cameraman Julio Macat twice before, first on the second unit of *Tango and Cash* and then again on *Home Alone 2*. Aggie, however, had not worked with Julio before, and they did not get along very well. Aggie and I filmed all the Los Angeles scenes and all the Washington D.C. scenes, but, after that, for some reason, Julio decided that Aggie had to go, so we were fired before they moved to North Carolina. As I have said before, this kind of thing happens in our business. It is no big deal. It is usually more about personality conflicts than ability.

As it turned out, this would eventually work to my advantage. One week later Laszlo called Aggie about a show he was starting called *My Best Friend's Wedding* to be filmed in Chicago. While we were in Chicago, I was able to visit my ill cousin Christine in Racine, Wisconsin and bring her a spring bouquet of flowers, she loved flowers. A few weeks later, she passed away, and I was able to attend her funeral. If we had still been on *My Fellow Americans,* I would have been in Asheville, North Carolina, and would not have been able to visit with my favorite cousin before she died or be able to go to her funeral. Thank you, Julio!

My Fellow American – The Lighting Crew
and Shooting on Locations

**In the Oval Office set Aggie, behind the desk,
(crew LtoR) Colin MacDonald, Matthew Hawkins,
John Haselbusch Paul Caven, Leroy Hershkowitz**

Scouting the Biltmore Estate in Ashville, North Carolina

Filming in Washington D.C.

229

PAUL CAVEN

MY BEST FRIEND'S WEDDING (1996)

Starring:	Julia Roberts, Dermot Mulroney, Cameron Diaz, Rupert Everett
Director:	P.J. Hogan
Cinematographer:	Laszlo Kovacs
Chief Lighting Technician:	Aggie Aguilar
Chief Rigging Technician:	Paul Caven (screen credit)

We filmed for five months in and around Chicago from May through September 1996. We filmed many of the Chicago landmarks, including the legendary Drake Hotel, in the chaos of O'Hare Airport on Labor Day weekend, as well as Union Station, at The Union League Club, on a tour boat on the Chicago River, and the wedding scenes at the landmark Fourth Presbyterian Church. We filmed after hours at Marshall-Fields Department Store, in Charlie Trotter's Restaurant, Buddy Guy's night club, and at Comiskey Park during a White Sox game. We filmed at the (now closed) Crab Shack, and we filmed the wedding reception scenes for three weeks at the Cuneo Mansion.

I was not Aggie's best boy on this film; rather, I was the rigging gaffer. I was hired as the best boy, but when we got to Chicago, the union local said I could not be the best boy. I had to be the rigging gaffer because they had a guy who always works as the best boy for incoming shows. They did not really want me at all. Most productions do not bring a best boy or a rigging gaffer. It was only because I had worked with Aggie and Laszlo for years and was part of their deal that they conceded to allow me to stay as the rigging gaffer. Needless to say, I did not get along very well with the Chicago best boy. I got along great with my Chicago rigging crew. The rigging crew comes ahead of the shooting crew and rigs the sets. Then that rigging crew comes back after they shoot it and strikes the sets. So, I was not on the set as much as I would be as the best boy and that, of course, was

230

their intent. What they did not stop to realize was that the rigging gaffer makes more money than the best boy.

This movie had a great cast. Julia Roberts was fabulous. She was funny and outgoing and really enjoyed this part. Cameron Diaz was very sweet and also very outgoing. I had worked with Dermot Mulroney twice before on the movies *Sunset* and *Copycat.* He was a wonderful guy and very friendly with the crew. This was my fifth show with M. Emmet Walsh. I probably worked with him more than any other supporting actor. I worked with him on *What's Up Doc, Nickelodeon, Sunset,* and *Free Willy 2,* but the actor who received most of the 26 awards for which this show was nominated or won was Rupert Everett. He won or was nominated for 11 awards.

I was not aware of it at the time, but this was my last film with Aggie before he retired. We worked together for 26 years, did over 40 movies, and countless commercials together. He was my mentor, my big brother, and is still my best friend. I look back with pride on the work we did on some classic films. We had a lot of good times and lots of laughs. I worked for another 10 years with plenty of good gaffers, but it was never the same without Aggie.

PAUL CAVEN

AS GOOD AS IT GETS (1997)

Starring: Jack Nicholson, Helen Hunt, Greg Kinnear, Cuba Gooding Jr., Shirley Knight

Director: James L. Brooks

Cinematographer: John Bailey

Chief Lighting
Technician: Mike Moyer

About half of this movie was filmed in New York; the rest was filmed in downtown Los Angeles and Long Beach, California. The interiors were filmed at Sony Studios. I was an extra guy on the crew and only worked on the local shooting in January and February 1997. The original working title was *Old Friends,* which I thought did not make much sense. Later they changed the title to a line that Jack Nicholson has as he is leaving his psychiatrist's office. He comments to the patients sitting in the waiting room, "This is as good as it gets"... in my opinion, a much better title.

This was a great movie. Jack and Helen Hunt both won Academy Awards and Golden Globe Awards. Greg Kinnear was nominated for both an Academy Award and a Golden Globe Award, and the film was also nominated or won 57 other awards world-wide. Cuba Gooding did a magnificent job as Greg Kinnear's artist's agent/manager. I had worked with Shirley Knight in 1975 on a TV movie called *Friendly Persuasion.*

This was my last picture with Jack Nicholson. It was fun working with him again. When he first saw me on the set, he pulled his sunglasses down to the end of his nose, looked at me, and said, "Haaay Paulie, how ya' been?" Jack is the best! Helen Hunt, on the other hand, was not very friendly. Giving her the benefit of the doubt, this was a very difficult role for her, and sometimes actors are so concerned about their performance that they forget to be nice to the people they should be nice to.

Verdell, the dog, was played by six different Brussels Griffons, named Timer the Dog, Sprout, Debbie, Billy the Dog, Parfait, and Jill the Dog. Jill was the star. In one scene, Jill the Dog starts mimicking Jack's character by stepping over the cracks in the sidewalk. They accomplished this by placing little obstacles on the cracks so that the dog had to step over them. They then removed the obstacles digitally in post-production.

The Director, James L. Brooks, is a very prolific writer, producer, and director. As a writer, he has won 19 Prime Time Emmy awards - more than any person in history at that time. As a producer, he won 9 Prime Time Emmy's, mostly for writing and producing *The Simpsons*. He won three Academy Awards for *Terms of Endearment*, he won 40 other Awards world-wide and was nominated 55 times. He is very good-natured with a very loud, boisterous laugh.

This was my second film with the cameraman John Bailey and his gaffer Mike (Moishe) Moyer. I worked briefly on a movie they did in 1989 called, *My Blue Heaven*. I would do four other shows with Moishe. I was hired because one of their regular guys, Devik Wiener, who was a friend of mine and worked with Aggie and me on several shows, recommended me.

As Good As It Gets - The Lighting Crew

The Lighting Crew
(LtoR) Randy Lewis, Michael Bonnaud, Paul Caven, Johnny O'Neil,
Jack Johnson, Mike Moyer, David Parks, David Burnett

SPHERE (1997)

Starring:	Dustin Hoffman, Sharon Stone, Samuel L. Jackson, Peter Coyote, Liev Schreiber, Queen Latifah
Director:	Barry Levinson
Cinematographer:	Adam Greenberg
Chief Lighting Technician:	Steve McGee

I worked on this movie from February through May 1997. It was filmed at the abandoned Mare Island Naval Shipyard in Vallejo, California. I did not work on the shooting crew; I was part of what is called the fixture crew. We fabricated, installed, and repaired all the light fixtures seen on the set. We rigged all the wall lights, the floor lights, and every light you see in the film. It was a very technical job because we not only had to fabricate many of the light fixtures, we had to make them all water proof so as not to electrocute anyone.

Once again, I was recommended for this job by a good friend of mine, Kevin Lang, who was the best boy and had worked with Aggie and me on many shows. Kevin first worked with us on *Mask* at Universal Studios. He was a regular there as a rigging gaffer and had a pretty steady job. After he rigged our sets on *Mask*, we got him on the shooting crew. He was such a good worker that Aggie and I asked him to leave his steady job at Universal and come with us on our next show, *Quicksilver,* at Warner Brothers. It was a very tough career decision for Kevin, but he decided to leave Universal, basically burning that bridge, to come with us. We, of course, as I have chronicled earlier, ended up getting fired off that show, leaving Kevin and the rest of my crew un-employed right before Christmas. Fortunately, we were able to hire him again on our next show, *Legal Eagles,* which was filmed at Universal Studios, so Kevin was able to come back to Universal with his head held high. He worked with us on many other shows, including being able to come with us to Spain on *Navy Seals* as our rigging gaffer. He has gone on to have a great career after that and never regretted leaving Universal.

The screenplay was adapted from a book by the award-winning Michael Crichton, known mostly for *Jurassic Park* and the TV show *ER*. The director, the award-winning Barry Levinson, was known for directing such blockbusters as *The Natural, Good Morning Vietnam, Rainman,* and *Bugsy.* This film, however, never won any awards. It pretty much bombed. Dustin Hoffman later would say how disappointed he was with the film.

The movie was filmed in warehouses with specially constructed water tanks rather than being filmed on the high seas because Warner Brothers did not want to repeat the debacle of *Waterworld.* Filming it on the ocean would have sent the budget into the stratosphere, which is what crippled *Waterworld's* chances at the box-office. They managed to trim the budget by 20 million dollars, but despite all of the budget cutting, *Sphere* still died a quiet death at the box-office.

The cinematographer, Adam Greenberg, is Israeli and speaks with a heavy accent. He is not what you might call genteel to his crew. If you happened to do something he did not like, he would holler at you in his thick Israeli accent yelling, "What are you doing, stupid boy?" Needless to say, he had a hard time keeping a crew. As I said, I was not on the shooting crew so I had very little contact with him on this film. I would work with him one other time on the shooting crew of *Rush Hour* with, not surprisingly, a different gaffer.

PAUL CAVEN

MIDNIGHT IN THE GARDEN OF GOOD AND EVIL (1997)

Starring: John Cusack, Kevin Spacey, Jack Thompson

Director: Clint Eastwood

Cinematographer: Jack Green

Chief Lighting
Technician: Tom Stern

Chief Rigging
Technician: Paul Caven (screen credit)

I did not work on the location filming in Savannah, Georgia; I only did the Los Angeles filming from June through July of 1997. I was recommended for the job by the Los Angeles best boy Frankie Jimenez, who had worked with Aggie and me on several shows. Clint Eastwood prefers using San Francisco crews on his films, if he can. He was able to use San Francisco people in Savannah, but when he came back to Los Angeles to shoot at Warner Brothers Studios, he had to use Hollywood people.

This was another quirky movie from Clint Eastwood. He always seems to pick the odd scripts. Clint is an excellent director; he knows what he wants and knows when he sees it. And when he sees what he wants, he prints it. He does not shoot take after take after take.

The movie was loosely based on a true story of a famous murder in Savannah, Georgia, and the tale of Jim Williams a Savannah antique dealer. Sonny Seiler, who plays the judge in the movie, was the real-life defense attorney on the original trial. (His pet bulldog, Uga, is the mascot for the University of Georgia Bulldogs.) Kevin Spacey (who plays Jim Williams) does an incredible job with this character. He not only puts on a convincing southern accent; he nails this character. This was my second film with John Cusack. We worked with him on *Say Anything*. He did a good job on this film, but his character was just an observer of the sub-plot. He did not have a lot of acting to do.

ALWAYS OUTNUMBERED (1997)

Starring:	Laurence Fishburne, Daniel Williams, Bill Cobbs, Natalie Cole, Cicely Tyson
Director:	Michael Apted
Cinematographer:	John Bailey
Chief Lighting Technician:	Michael Moyer
Lighting Technician:	Paul Caven (screen credit)

This was an HBO movie that we filmed from September to October 1997 in and around Los Angeles. This was the same cinematographer, gaffer, and lighting crew that I had worked with a few months before on the movie *As Good As It Gets.*

The book and the screenplay were written by Walter Mosley. Walter was on the set most of the time and was a very friendly guy. He gave the crew autographed hardbound copies of his book, *Always Outnumbered, Always Outgunned.* Laurence Fishburne was fantastic. I had worked with him before on *Quicksilver.* It was terrific to be able to work with such well-known character actors as Bill Cobb and Cicely Tyson. Natalie Cole was charming; she was very friendly with the crew.

One late Friday night, we were filming the emotional final scene on a bus stop bench in the predominantly black Crenshaw district of Los Angeles. A few hundred feet away was a very loud, boisterous neighborhood bar. The noise was ruining our sound takes. They sent the young, very white, female second assistant director over to ask them to hold it down. After they laughed her out of the joint, we thought we were just going to have to put up with the noise and loop (record) the sound later. When they told Laurence about the problem he said, "Let me see what I can do," and he headed for the bar. As soon as he walked in the door, the place fell silent. He told them if they would keep the noise down for a half an hour, he would come back after we wrapped and buy the house a round. We got our shots done, and we all went home, and the folks in the bar got to party with Laurence Fishburne. A win, win!

Always Outnumbered - The Cast

Lawrence Fishburne's Good Wishes

Natalie Cole's Good Wishes

RUSH HOUR (1997)

Starring:	Jackie Chan, Chris Tucker, Ken Leung, Elizabeth Peña, Tom Wilkinson, Tzi Ma
Director:	Brett Ratner
Cinematographer:	Adam Greenberg
Chief Lighting Technician:	Robert Jason

We filmed this movie from November to December of 1997. I was a lighting technician on this film, and I was hired once again by my friend Frankie Jimenez, who was the best boy. I knew the gaffer as well. I had worked with his father Gene Jason years before at Warner Brothers. I remember Bobby coming to visit his dad when he was a little kid. Bobby was as pleasant as his father was and has become an excellent gaffer. We filmed at various Los Angeles locations, Grumman's Chinese Theater in Hollywood, a house in Pasadena, the Doheny Graystone Mansion, the Foo-Chow Restaurant in Chinatown, and the ill-fated Ambassador Hotel, where Bobby Kennedy was killed, which was condemned at the time due to earthquake damage and has since been demolished.

Jackie Chan was a lot of fun to work with. He was just like another guy on the crew. He has a great sense of humor and was always laughing and joking with the guys, although his English was sometimes challenging. He had an entourage of a dozen Chinese stunt guys. It was fun to watch them lay out a stunt. They would all group around Jackie and chatter away in Chinese and then they would all move simultaneously like a swarm of bees to another spot and chatter some more. Then they would all dance over to another spot. Well, whatever they were talking about worked. Jackie did some really great stunts, everything from phenomenal martial arts fight scenes to a couple of very dangerous high falls.

I was not as impressed with Chris Tucker as Chris Tucker was impressed with himself. He made the prop guy set up a full-length mirror everywhere he went so he could check out his looks and his moves. He spends half the movie talking in a falsetto whine. Apparently, Eddie Murphy turned the part down, and that was too bad because I think they ended up with a poor excuse for an Eddie Murphy wanna-be. He never knew his lines, most of his dialog ended up being improvised, which is always a great help to your fellow actors who are waiting for a scripted cue line.

I had worked with the cameraman, Adam Greenberg, earlier in the year on *Sphere*. As I mentioned before, Adam was not an easy person to work for. He would get angry and yell at people. He asked me to fabricate several huge "china ball" lights that he wanted to use. I designed, and had the studio welding shop make me, 4 metal framed balls, 4 feet in diameter with a bracket in the middle for me to use to mount a 10,000-watt socket with a 10,000-watt bulb. I then wrapped them with a white, light-softening material. He liked what I did and liked my work, so he never yelled at me. You can see the huge china balls I made in the final stunt sequence that we filmed at the Los Angeles Convention Center.

THE OUT-OF-TOWNERS (1998)

Starring: Steve Martin, Goldie Hawn, John Cleese

Director: Sam Weisman

Cinematographer: John Bailey

Chief Lighting
Technician: Mike Moyer

Lighting Technician: Paul Caven (screen credit)

This was my third film with Mike (Moishe) Moyer and his crew. I would end up doing five movies with Moishe. Almost all of the guys on his crew had worked with Aggie and me through the years. I did not work on any of the New York shooting; I only worked on the Los Angeles shooting. We filmed this movie from February to May of 1998. We filmed at Paramount Studios and around the Los Angeles area: at the Los Angeles Convention Center (again), Los Angeles Union Station, LAX Airport, and the John Wayne Airport in Orange County.

It was wonderful working with Goldie Hawn again. I had worked with her on *Shampoo* and *Swing Shift.* She is an enjoyable person, and she has an infectious laugh and laughs a lot. She is a free spirit. I had worked with Steve Martin three years earlier on *Father of the Bride II.* I mentioned before that he was not very outgoing with the crew, and he had not changed. John Cleese, on the other hand, was a "hoot." This *Monty Python* veteran was incredibly witty. We would joke with him about skits like "the ministry of silly walks," and he would do it for us. He would go through the whole routine. It was hilarious.

This was a remake of the Neil Simon movie with the same name from 1970 with Jack Lemmon and Sandy Dennis. This version did not do very well in the box office; it had a 78-million-dollar budget but only grossed 28.5 million dollars. This was my second Neil Simon movie. I worked on his movie, *The Cheap Detective.* Neil Simon originally intended *The Out of Towners* to be a segment of the play *Plaza Suite.* It was entitled Visitor from Toledo and was intended to open the play on Broadway but was cut during the rehearsal period. Simon wrote this for the screen after realizing that a play would have difficulty portraying the many different locations involved.

241

The Out of Towners - The Crew

The Crew Collage
(Photo credit: Marsha Blackburn)

NEVER BEEN KISSED (1998)

Starring: Drew Barrymore, David Arquette, Michael Vartan, Molly Shannon, John C. Reilly, Gary Marshall

Director: Raja Gosnell

Cinematographer: Alex Nepomniaschy

Chief Lighting
Technician: Mike Moyer

Lighting Technician: Paul Caven (screen credit)

The screen credits on this film were unique. As we were finishing the movie, they asked the crew to submit their dorkiest high school age picture to use in the credits. They added all the crew pictures to the end credits. You can see my photo in the credits; I am the cute, little, blonde kid with the accordion in my lap. Don't ask!

We filmed this movie from June to September of 1998. They filmed a few scenes in Chicago, but the majority of the film was filmed in and around Los Angeles. The school scenes were filmed in John Burroughs Middle School in Hollywood. We were there, of course, during the summer when school was out. The athletic field was at William S. Hart High School in Newhall, California. The baseball field was the Jackie Robinson Field in Westwood where the U.C.L.A. baseball team plays. The prom scenes were filmed at the Wilshire Ebell main ballroom.

The director, Raja Gosnell, was an editor turned director. He edited *Home Alone II: Lost in New York.* He was also the son of Ray Gosnell, who was the assistant director on *Paper Moon* and *What's Up Doc.* Raja was 14 years old back then.

The actors were friendly. Drew Barrymore was pleasant to work with. David Arquette was delightful, and so was John C. Reilly. Gary Marshall, of course, was a veteran actor, director, and producer. He was a very amusing person, and he would make hilarious comments and joke around. When he walked in a room, everything would stop. He was always the center of attention. He had a very loud voice, so it was easy to be the center of attention. In one scene, Garry Marshall's character is speaking to his employees at the Chicago Sun-Times board room, he says in frustration, "I don't even know my own kids." His real-life daughter, Kathleen Marshall, is sitting to his right in that scene.

Drew's character, Josie, is a reporter for the Chicago Sun Times. Gary Marshall gives her the assignment to go back to High School and to write a news story about it. Josie's assignment resembles the experiences of Cameron Crowe, who went back to his old high school at 21 and wrote a novel and screenplay based on his experience there, which eventually became the movie *Fast Times at Ridgemont High.*

Never Been Kissed – The Cast and Crew

Photo: Suzanne Hanover/SMPSP

NEVER BEEN KISSED
SUMMER 1998
The Cast and Crew (Photo Credit: Suzanne Hanover)

Paul Caven's Screen Credit Photo
(Photo Credit: Class photo from Milton Mann Accordion Studios)

PAUL CAVEN

FOR LOVE OF THE GAME (1999)

Starring:	Kevin Costner, Kelly Preston, John C. Reilly, Jena Malone, and Vin Scully
Director:	Sam Raimi
Cinematographer:	John Bailey
Chief Lighting Technician:	Mike Moyer
Lighting Technician:	Paul Caven (screen credit)

We filmed from December 1998 through February 1999. I did not work on any of the New York filming. They filmed the game sequence at Yankee Stadium, but the dugout scenes were at Dodger Stadium, and the scenes with Vin Scully and Steve Lyons were filmed on stage at Universal Studios. We filmed at the Los Angeles Convention Center, USC, Long Beach, Marina Del Rey, and Aspen, Colorado. This was my last film with Mike Moyer and John Bailey.

The biggest thrill I had on this movie was being able to sit and talk Dodger baseball with the Hall of Fame Dodger announcer Vin Scully. Vinny was ranked #1 by the American Sportscasters Association in its list of the Top 50 Sportscasters of all-time (January 2009). He has called four perfect games in his career, including Sandy Koufax's perfect game in 1965. He was wonderful, a class act, and a real gentleman. There is nothing he loves more than baseball. He would not go to his dressing room between shots; he would stay on stage and talk with us for hours between shooting. He's the best!

Steve Lyons, a former player who plays Vin Scully's broadcast partner, did end up being a Dodger announcer in 2005. However, he is probably most infamous for his "pants down" incident in Detroit, 1990, when, during a game, he unbuttoned and dropped his pants in an effort to shake dirt out of them after diving into first base.

The Director, Sam Raimi, was best known for directing *Spider Man 1, 2* and *3*. He was a TV producer turned director. I had just worked with John C. Reilly a few months earlier on *Never Been*

246

Kissed. As I mentioned before, I had worked with Kevin Costner before on one of his first movies, *Frances.*

The shots of Billy Chapel's parents at the beginning of the movie are Kevin Costner's actual parents. The scene in which the ball bounces off of Mickey Hart's head is based on the famous incident in which the same thing happened to Texas Rangers outfielder Jose Canseco. Afterward, when Billy and Mickey are talking in the clubhouse, Mickey jokes "It'll probably end up on ESPN." In fact, Canseco's incident became blooper reel fodder on ESPN for the remainder of that year.

All four umpires were played by real Major League umpires. Many of the Yankees players were played by Yankee minor leaguers. Most of the spectators in the stands were "virtual" cardboard people that they propped up in the seats. They work cheap, and they don't need a lunch break. The house we filmed in Aspen was Kevin's house.

Jena Malone, who plays Kelly Preston's daughter, was 14 years old at the time and was nominated for a Blockbuster Entertainment Award, a Young Artist Award, and a Young Star Award. Kevin Costner was nominated for a Razzi Award for Worst Actor. As a matter of fact, Kevin has been nominated or won 11 Razzi awards over the years. In all fairness, he has also won an Academy Award, has been nominated or won several other awards, mostly just for one movie, *Dancing With Wolves.*

As a side note related to the industry, *Dances with Wolves* was filmed non-union with a mostly union crew that was forced to work for no benefits. This sort of thing happened a lot on non-union independent films. They would usually pay more, but the extra pay did not buy your health care or donate to your pension. Non-union also means you work with none of the guaranteed union working conditions in regard to working hours or number of hours off between shifts or the living conditions on location. Most union people did not do a lot of these shows.

The title page drawing in this book was done by Earl Benton. He was the "stand-by painter" on the shooting company. They always have a stand-by painter on the set to do touch ups. He is also a very talented artist. His specialty is drawing his subjects candidly, with humor, and viewed from behind. The people in the drawing are all on the lighting crew, and they cannot figure out why the light is not on.

247

It is uncanny how he can convey personal characteristics that identify each person. The four "juicers" in the drawing (from left to right) are Me, Johnny O'Neil, Kenny Ballantine, and Dave Parks. Thanks, Earl. I had the picture framed and it is hanging on my wall... it is one of my treasures. I am including it here, again, because I love it so.

The "Juicers"
(LtoR) Paul Caven, Johnny O'Neil, Kenny Ballantine, & Dave Parks

For Love of the Game – The Crew and Shooting on Location

**The Lighting Crew
(LtoR) Johnny O'Neil, Kenny Balentine,
David Burnett, Paul Caven, Ron Ash**

Shooting in the Snow

More Shooting in the Snow

ACTION (1999)

Starring:	Jay Mohr, Illeana Douglas, Jarrad Paul, Jack Plotnick, Buddy Hackett, Lee Arenberg
Director:	Various Directors
Cinematographer:	Paul Maibaum
Chief Lighting Technician:	Gary Haselbusch

This project was a short-lived TV series made for Fox TV. Gary Haselbusch and I knew each other, but I had never worked for him before. I got this job as a lighting technician because Gary's son, John Haselbusch, was the best boy, and I had hired Johnny several times on shows with Aggie and me. Johnny hired several other guys that had worked for Aggie and me. We filmed this series from August through December of 1999. We filmed several local locations, but all the stage work was done at Culver Studios in Culver City, California.

The show was originally intended to air on HBO, with Oliver Platt instead of Jay Mohr as Peter Dragon. Fox TV was offered the show to try to leverage HBO to provide more money. HBO wanted to pick up the series, but creators Chris Thompson and Joel Silver elected to go with Fox's higher-budget instead. Fox ended up airing only 8 shows before the series was canceled, with the remaining 5 episodes left to air on the FX cable network instead.

I thought the show was comical. Maybe it was a little too campy, too "Hollywood" for the average viewer. I thought the situations that came up were so true to life in Hollywood that it made me laugh. The series chronicles the trials and tribulations of a producer, Peter Dragon, played by Jay Mohr, making a movie titled, *Beverly Hills Gun Club.* It goes through the entire process from buying the screenplay, to hiring a director, to hiring the lead actors, and shooting the movie.

The characters of Peter Dragon and Bobby D. (Lee Arenberg) are loosely based on real-life Hollywood heavyweights Joel Silver (who is an executive producer of this series) and Barry Diller. The series does not have a very good ending because they were counting on carrying it on into a new season. The plan was to do a season that showed the making of *Beverly Hills Gun Club* and then actually show the finished movie on Fox. That did not happen… they were canceled. The show did, however, win a Golden Satellite Award for Best Television Series, plus Jay Mohr and Illeana Douglas both won Golden Satellite Awards for Best Performance.

Jay Mohr was quirky; he is a stand-up comedian, so most of the time we were just another one of his audiences. He would come on stage and start his act as he walked through the crew. He was mostly amusing, but sometimes he would make Buddy Hackett the butt of his jokes, and the crew did not like that.

We all liked Buddy better than we liked Jay, so we would not laugh at his "Buddy" jokes. Buddy Hackett had forgotten more about comedy than Jay would ever know. It was such an honor to work with Buddy Hackett, but this show was at the end of his illustrious career. He was 75 years old and would pass away only four years later. I cannot say it often enough, and this is a perfect example, of how the old-time actors, as opposed to the new crop, relate to the crew as co-workers not as their minions.

The production was able to get a pretty impressive cast of day players, at least at first. (A day player is an actor who is not a regular on a show and only works a few days on a show. They are on a Day Players Contract.) Later on, they were not able to get the big names. Keanu Reeves was in the pilot. Salma Hayek was in episode 2. Sandra Bullock was in episode 4. David Hasselhoff was in episode 5. By episode 6, they were down to Scott Wolf and Tony Hawk. By the time we got to episode 10, all they could get was David Leisure (Joe Isuzu), and he did not even get a screen credit.

The End of Another Decade

By the end of 1999 the Second Golden Era was pretty much over. Most of the original big five studios: Warner Bros., Paramount, 20th Century Fox, Disney and Universal studios were now owned by multi-national corporations like Viacom, Comcast, Sony and Warner Media. This new source of income and marketing muscle gave the studios a shot in the arm. Independent producers were now able to distribute their product through many more avenues than ever before without the studios. Streaming companies like HBO, Cinemax, and Netflix were producing their own content now.

Lighting was on the threshold of another evolution including the advent of lighting computer consoles, moving lights, and the use of LED lights. After the fiasco that happened with the change from DC to AC, The Motion Pictures Producers Association with the assistance of our union, Local 728 I.A.T.S.E, started a comprehensive, required training program. Today the program has grown and expanded to include all of the new technology.

CHAPTER 5 - THE 21ST CENTURY

THE HOME STRETCH

SIX FEET UNDER (2000-2005)

Starring:	Peter Krause, Michael C. Hall, Frances Conroy, Lauren Ambrose, Freddy Rodriguez, Mathew St. Patrick, Rachel Griffiths, Richard Jenkins
Director:	Various directors
Cinematographer:	Alan Caso (2001-2004), Jim Denault (2005) and various other cinematographers
Chief Lighting Technician:	Roger Sassen (2001-2004), Skip McCraw (2005)

I was hired to be the rigging gaffer on this show in October of 2000. I had never worked for Roger Sassen before, but he knew Aggie. A friend of mine, Devik Wiener, was working with Roger at the time on a show he was finishing up. Roger mentioned that he needed a rigging gaffer to start rigging their new show *Six Feet Under* while they finished the show they were on. Devik suggested me. He mentioned that I was Aggie's best boy, and I was hired sight unseen.

I rigged all the permanent sets. They wanted all the sets hooked up to be dimmer controlled with a console dimmer system, a fairly new concept for film. Up until then, dimmer control systems were mostly used in stage plays and live audience shows. I was almost finished getting everything set up when Roger told me that they could not carry a rigging gaffer for the rest of the show, so the only way he could keep me on was if I could be the dimmer console operator. I had no idea how to operate the dimmer console. Designing and rigging a dimmer system and programming and operating a dimmer console are two entirely different skills. I was signed up to take dimmer classes through our union local, but the classes did not start for another 3 or 4 weeks. I barely knew how to turn the board on. So I of course told him, "Sure. OK." I then called in a friend of mine to give me a crash course, and I faked my way through the first few weeks. Years later I confessed my lie to Roger and he just laughed and said he would have done the same thing.

Computer software is available to use to create a lighting plot for a particular set. The lighting plot shows where every light is placed on the set, the dimmer number it is plugged in to, the direction it is pointing, if it has a color on it and so forth. This being my first ever dimmer board show and not knowing my dimmer board future, I did not purchase that software or a laptop, I drew a lighting plot for each set by hand, old school. Roger borrowed one of my plot maps one day and unbeknownst to me he sent a copy into Lighting Dimensions magazine and they printed it in their April 2002 edition with an article about *Six Feet Under.* Roger told me he made sure the copy had my name on the bottom.

I worked on all five seasons. Roger Sassen only did the first four seasons. At the end of the fourth season, we knew the cameraman did not want to do the next season, so we assumed we would not be back either. I got along great with Roger and all of his crew. We did the first four seasons together, plus Roger hired me several times thereafter on other jobs. As a matter of fact, I was working for Roger on the last day of my last show before I retired.

Just before the start of the fifth season of *Six Feet Under,* I received a call from the production manager who wanted me to come back for the fifth season. He said because I rigged all the permanent sets, and was the dimmer board operator and knew all the set cues, he wanted me to do the fifth season. I did not get along very well with the gaffer on the fifth season, Skip McCraw. I am not sure why, possibly he knew I was hired before he was, but whatever the reason we did not get along. Skip was a young, fairly new gaffer at the time. He had not yet learned how to best use his crew's knowledge or experience. One time while filming on location, we rigged a couple of our big HMI lights in a 60-foot Condor aerial lift to light the scene. When it came time to send someone up in the Condor to operate the lights, Skip assigned me. You usually send one of your least experienced operators to sit up in a Condor. As I was on my way up in the Condor, I heard the key grip question Skip asking, "Why are you sending your most experienced man up in the Condor?" Skip just looked at him.

Six Feet Under was a ground-breaking HBO series. It not only dealt with death, it also dealt graphically with homosexuality. It became an immediate hit. Within a week of the first episode being aired, HBO renewed the show for a second season. One of the trademarks of the show was that each episode began with a scene where somebody dies. Then the rest of the show's back story was about the embalming and the funeral of the deceased while the real story was about the dysfunctional Fisher family. Over the five seasons, it won or was nominated for 8 Golden Globe Awards; it won another 46 national and international awards and was nominated for 117 more.

I started rigging the permanent sets in October of 2000 at the Sunset/Gower Studios. That lot used to be the Columbia Studio lot. It dates back to the 1920s. There were some classic films made there like, *It Happened One Night* with Clark Gable and Claudette Colbert in 1934. In the 1950s and 1960s they filmed some timeless TV shows like *Bewitched, I Dream of Jeannie* and *The Monkees.*

Our permanent sets were interiors of the Fisher home and funeral parlor. The exterior of the Fisher & Sons funeral home was actually the well-known Auguste R. Marquis residence in the West Adams District of Los Angeles, which now houses the Filipino Federation of America in Los Angeles. One of our other locations was Nikolai's flower shop. It was a working flower shop at 14325 Ventura Blvd in the San Fernando Valley. Prior to that, it was a gas station. It was, in fact, the gas station were James Dean filled up his Porsche "Spyder" the day he left town on his way to eternity. There is a color photo hung up in the office of him standing at the station that day, about to get back behind the wheel.

All of the actors on this show were very friendly. When you work with the same people for five years, 7 to 9 months out of the year, you get to be one big family. Peter and Michael were very pleasant. Frances

Conroy would always bring in a big plate of home-baked cookies or brownies whenever she worked. Richard Jenkins plays the father of the Fisher family. He dies in the pilot episode but reappears in several later episodes. I had just worked with Illeana Douglas on *Action*. She worked on several episodes. Kathy Bates directed some of the episodes and later acted in some episodes. She was very outgoing and friendly. Ed Begley Jr. played in several episodes. He was very sociable especially if you wanted to talk about "green energy." James Cromwell was one of my favorites on this show. He is a liberal California Democrat just like me, and we would talk politics. He was working on the show during the 2004 Presidential election, so we would have some heated discussions about the election.

Six Feet Under – The Crew

SEASON 2 CAST & CREW

The Crew Season 2
(Photo Credit: Unknown)

SEASON 5 CAST & CREW

The Crew Season 5
(Photo Credit: Unknown)

Six Feet Under – Lighting Plot

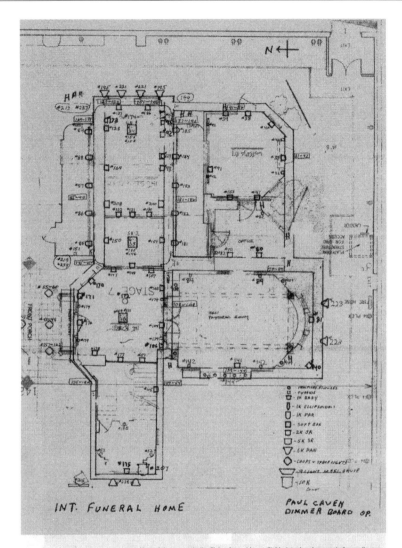

Most of the spaces in the Fisher funeral home (light plot, above) are part of a contiguous stage set at Sunset Gower Studios. The rig includes a large complement of Mole-Richardson studio lights, especially 2k juniors. Outside the windows are 5k skypans.

Caso also likes to use bounce light creatively.

Lighting Plot for Stage 7,
Funeral Home set
(Photo Credit. Lighting Dimensions Magazine, April 2002)

JAG (2003)

Starring:	David James Elliott, Patrick Labyorteaux, Catherine Bell, John M. Jackson
Director:	Various directors
Cinematographer:	Frank Perl
Chief Lighting Technician:	Roger Sassen

We did the ninth season of *JAG* just before we started Season 4 of *Six Feet Under*. We filmed from July through November of 2003 at the Valencia Studios. We took over from the lighting crew that did the first 8 seasons because they were jumping ship to start a new show being produced by the same company and being filmed at the same studio lot. They knew that *JAG* was close to being canceled (it only went one more season after ours), so they hopped on this new show hoping it would last more than one season. It turned out to be the right decision; the new show they started was called *NCIS*.

It is sometimes difficult to come onto a show that has been shooting for 8 seasons. I was the dimmer board operator, so I inherited a system designed by someone else. A system that had been hashed and re-hashed over the past eight years, but I had to work with it because there was no way to change it without re-doing it.

Catherine Bell was super friendly. She was the crew sweetheart. She would say "Hi" to everyone when she came on the set. David James Elliott was a different thing all together. He was not very well regarded. No one referred to him as David or James; they all just called him "Number One" because he was the star of the show and the number one name on the call sheet. In my opinion, he was kind of a jerk. Apparently, on an earlier season he decided to play a practical joke on one of the actors and snuck up behind camera with a hand gun filled with blanks and fired one off. He was standing right behind the grip that operates the camera dolly, and he brought the gun up right next to the dolly grips' ear when he pulled the trigger. Tragically the grip sustained permanent ear damage and is deaf in one ear to this day.

DR. VEGAS (2004)

Starring:	Rob Lowe, Sarah Lancaster, Lisa Gabriel, Joe Pantoliano, Tom Sizemore, Adam Clark, Amy Adams
Director:	Various Directors
Cinematographer:	Philip Holahan
Chief Lighting Technician:	Roger Sassen

This was another show I did with Roger Sassen after Season 4 of *Six Feet Under*. We filmed from August through October of 2004 mostly on stage at Columbia/Warner Brothers Ranch Lot in Burbank. This was a good show that I believe could have been a great show with a little more time for the characters to mature. CBS only aired 5 of the 10 episodes we shot. The story was about an emergency room doctor, played by Rob Lowe, who leaves the emergency room to take a job as an in-house doctor in a high-end hotel casino in Las Vegas.

Rob was great, a regular guy and a good actor. Amy Adams stole almost every scene she was in. She did a great job with her character. Rob and Joe Pantoliano made a great team. Joe was an accomplished actor. I had worked with him in 1973 when he had a small, uncredited part in *For Pete's Sake,* one of his first films. He became famous for his characterization of Ralph Cifaretto on *The Sopranos*. The critics did not like the show, they kept comparing it to the show *Las Vegas* that was a hit show at the time. The two shows were totally different, so it was really an unfair criticism.

Tom Sizemore was at a very bad place in his life at this time. He was quoted as saying "For years I fooled myself into thinking I could or even was getting off drugs. People knew I was using but they still hired me for their films. I was grateful back then, but it was what contributed to my downward spiral." He did pretty well on this show and he has since become clean and sober. (Source: Tom Sizemore Bio IMDb.com.)

MODERN MEN (2005)

Starring:	Eric Lively, Jane Seymour, Marla Sokoloff, Josh Braaten, Max Greenfield, George Wendt
Director:	Various Directors
Cinematographer:	Julius Metoyer
Chief Lighting Technician:	Jeff Strong

My good friend Devik Wiener, who got me the five-year long gig on *Six Feet Under,* suggested me for this dimmer board job too. The gaffer, Jeff Strong, worked with Aggie and me a couple of times. His brother, Chris Strong, also worked with us several times. The cinematographer, Julius Metoyer, and I got in the business around the same time and we had worked as electricians together in our "rookie years" at Warner Brothers in the 1960s. I could tell even then that Julius was going places.

We filmed this show at the Columbia/Warner Brothers Ranch lot from September through November of 2005. The show was filmed before a live audience, at least most of it was. These shows are different from other TV shows or movies; they are filmed more like a stage play. In movies and TV shows, they basically use only one camera and each scene is broken up into different camera angles which require the camera to be reset each time and relit each time. On a live audience show, they use four cameras at once, and the actors play the entire scene non-stop while the cameras move around to get the required camera angles. The other thing that makes it like live theater is that you work mostly at night. These shows only shoot three nights a week and only one of those nights is in front of the live audience. We would prep on Monday and then shoot the live show on Tuesday night. We would come in at around 11:00 am on Tuesday, get set up to shoot, shoot the live show from 7:00 pm until around 10:00 pm or so, then we would work till around 2:00 or 3:00 am re-vamping the set for the next night's shooting. Wednesday and Thursday nights, we would shoot without the audience, but we would still stay late after shooting to re-vamp the sets for the next night.

Jane Seymour was the only actor I knew on this show, and that was part of the problem. Jane Seymour was the only actor anyone knew. She was delightful and a very good actress, but it takes more than one good actor to have a successful show. This show only filmed seven episodes.

BECAUSE I SAID SO (2006)

Starring:	Diane Keaton, Mandy Moore, Gabriel Macht, Tom Everett Scott, Lauren Graham, Piper Perabo, Stephen Collins
Director:	Michael Lehmann
Cinematographer:	Julio Macat
Chief Lighting Technician:	Bob Krattiger
Rigging Electrician:	Paul Caven (screen credit)

I was hired and received screen credit as a rigging electrician. I worked with the rigging crew to set up and strike the sets (the rigging gaffer, Wally Nichols, was an old friend of mine), but on days when there was no rigging to be done, I would work with the shooting crew. I knew the best boy and all the guys on the crew. They had all worked for me at one time or another. I had worked with the gaffer's father, Bill Krattiger, when I first started at Warner Brothers. I had also worked with the cameraman, Julio Macat, about 10 year earlier when he fired Aggie and me on *My Fellow Americans.* I am not sure if he recognized me, but I just stayed under the radar and kept a low profile.

This was my third and last film with Diane Keaton. She was delightful and a very accomplished actress winning dozens of awards, including Academy Awards, Golden Globe Awards and many more for such films as *Annie Hall, Looking for Mr. Goodbar, Reds,* and *The Godfather* I, II, and III.

In this film, there is a scene where Diane and her three daughters go for a massage. Diane refuses to take off her clothes for the massage, and the girls all tease her for it. It is funny because one of Diane's first roles was in the Broadway play *Hair,* which was infamous for its final scene where the actors all get nude; well not all the actors; Diane famously refused to take her clothes off. At least she is consistent.

Mandy Moore was lovely. She did a lot of singing and voice over work. She is best known for *The Princess Diaries, A Walk to*

Remember, Saved, and as the voice of Rapunzel in *Tangled.* Lauren Graham was best known for *The Gilmore Girls,* which I had worked on with Roger from time to time as an extra man.

RAINES (2006)

Starring:	Jeff Goldblum, Matt Craven, Nichole Sullivan, Linda Park, Dov Davidoff, Malik Yoba, Luis Guzman
Director:	Frank Darabont
Cinematographer:	Oliver Bokelberg
Chief Lighting Technician:	Roger Sassen

This was a TV Pilot we filmed in March of 2006. Roger hired me again as a dimmer board operator/lamp operator. We only filmed the Pilot (3 days of prep and 10 days of shooting). They went on to shoot 6 other episodes until NBC pulled the plug. I thought it was an interesting show, and it had a unique concept. Jeff Goldblum plays a homicide detective who, during murder investigations, gets a little help from the ghost of the victim. It was kind of cool the way they filmed the ghost scenes. The cinematographer, Oliver Bokelberg, was nominated by the American Society of Cinematographers for Outstanding Achievement for his work on this Pilot.

Jeff Goldblum was delightful and very friendly. He has appeared in over a hundred shows, and has been nominated or won over a dozen different film awards.

Luis Guzmán originally had the role of Charlie Lincoln, but after the pilot was filmed, he was replaced by Malik Yoba. NBC then asked that the producers re-shoot the scenes in which Luis appeared.

PAUL CAVEN

TELL ME YOU LOVE ME (2006)

Starring:	Michelle Borth, Tim DeKay, Aislinn Paul, Adam Scott, Sonya Walger, Ally Walker, Jane Alexander
Director:	Various Directors
Cinematographer:	Alan Caso
Chief Lighting Technician:	Roger Sassen

Right after I completed filming of *Raines* in March of 2006, my wife and I sold our house in La Cañada, California, and moved to Gallatin, Missouri. A couple of years earlier we bought a 46-acre farm and planned on building our dream home in rural America. We started construction in April, and in September of 2006 Roger called and asked if I wanted to do one last show with him. I could not officially retire until January of 2007, so I said yes and flew back to Los Angeles.

This was an HBO series and contained some pretty graphic sex scenes. In an interview with "The A.V. Club," Adam Scott said that his contract for this show was very specific about what kind of and how much nudity he would have to show.

The actors were all pleasant; probably the nicest was Jane Alexander. Of course, she is a pro. She has had a long and illustrious career. It was great working with Ronny Cox again. I had not worked with him since *Deliverance* in 1971. He was as gracious as ever; a real gentleman.

The show got pretty good ratings so the series was renewed for a second season, but creator Cynthia Mort decided not to continue the series. She felt that she was not able to create enough stories for a second season. Why would you create a TV series with only one season in mind? There is not a writer in Hollywood that would not jump at the opportunity of coming up with enough stories for a season two of a hit series; well, maybe there is one.

I worked on the show from September through November 2006. We filmed in and around the Los Angeles area and on stage at CBS

Studios in Studio City. Just before Thanksgiving, they told us they would be going on hiatus until the first week in January. I would be retired by then, so I would not be coming back on the show.

My last day in the motion picture industry would be on stage 12 at CBS Studios on November 20, 2006. That afternoon on the set they stopped shooting and called me to the set from my dimmer room. They had a cake for me saying "Happy Retirement," and the first assistant director, Venita Ozols, gave a very nice speech about the first time we worked together.

Venita was a rookie second assistant director on *On Golden Pond.* Her primary job was to be a liaison between the production and the transportation department. The problem was that the Boston Teamsters on the show, some of whom had just gotten out of jail, did not like the idea of taking orders from a woman! Venita handled the situation with her trademark smile and a great attitude, so she gained the respect of the crew. Her positive attitude moved her up the ladder to become the person who is in charge on the set, the first assistant director.

I thanked Venita and with a retrospective view I said, "I am so grateful for having a magnificent career, working with such brilliant, creative people through the years, but I thankfully pass the torch to a new generation of film makers." (They, of course, were all too young to know where I plagiarized that phrase from) "After 40 years, 3 months and 14 days," I continued, "I think I have enough memories to last a lifetime. I'm headed for the rocking chair on the front porch of my farm in Missouri. So I wish for all of you, the good fortune I enjoyed as well as a career you can be proud of."

After we wrapped, I had a wrap beer with Roger and the guys. I thanked Roger for hiring me so often after Aggie retired. He was a godsend to me at a time when I was not working a lot. I wished everyone good luck and started the final slow walk back to the parking garage. As I walked through the darkness between the towering stages of the "Dream Factory," I could not help but think back on the last 40 years of my life. I returned to that afternoon on Warner Brothers back lot with *Rin Tin Tin*, and thinking that this would be fun.

Well, it was not only fun, it was a wonderful life and I would not change a day of it. I had an amazing career. I had the good fortune of getting hooked up with an incredible gaffer like Aggie and working on some classic independent films of the 1970s and 1980s, an era later to be deemed "Hollywood's Second Golden Age of Movies." We worked with some award-winning cinematographers and directors throughout the years. I got the opportunity to travel the world, see places I would never have seen otherwise, meet people I would never have met otherwise, and forged lifelong friendships.

As I drove through the studio gate for the very last time, I waved to the security guard. He smiled and said, "Good night, Mr. Caven." I stopped for a moment, looked at him, smiled, and thought to myself, "No, it's good bye."

EPILOGUE

I have to admit it still gives me a thrill seeing my name come up on the silver screen, no matter how small the text or how fast it rolls by; it is like a little piece of immortality. I loved my job. I always did my best, and I was always proud of my contribution to the collectively creative process of making movies.

We all contribute our part no matter how small. We all make our mark. It is like the old joke about the guy in the circus parade walking behind the elephants sweeping up the droppings. They ask him, "Why would you want a job like that? How can you do that? Why don't you quit?" He answers, "What, and give up show business?"

The movie business is not all sunglasses and autographs. It was wonderful to have the opportunity to travel, and I enjoyed the experience, but that also means you spend a lot of lonely nights in hotel rooms in the middle of nowhere. Life on the road gets to be a drag, living out of a suit case, traveling from town to town, and missing the ones you love.

Sometimes, I would be on distant location for six to nine months out of the year. Being away so much means we are not home for some of the milestones of our families' lives. Luckily, Denise, and later Danielle, sometimes traveled to my location and were with me for a few weeks at a time. They were even able to travel for part of the time with me in Spain on *Navy Seals*. But, most of the time, it was me having a couple of beers with the guys in the hotel bar after work then a long, lonely night in my room alone.

Sometimes I would call Denise just to hear her say "Hello." I would look out my window at the moon and ask her if she was looking at the moon. She would say yes, and it would feel like we were closer because we were both looking at the same moon. She, of course, was just as lonely as me, plus she had the responsibility of taking care of Danielle by herself. Denise understood the business and knew what had to be done in this business to make a living. She had spent enough time on locations to understand how it works. Denise was the best "Crew Wife" ever.

They say "Hollywood marriages never last." I believe a big part of the reason is not because of infidelity or disinterest; it is because the spouse does not understand the business of making movies. They become suspicious, they do not believe that you are working 14, 16, or 18 hours a day. It is difficult for them to deal with the fact some weeks you may start work at 6:00 am on Monday morning, and by Friday you are starting at 6:00 pm and will be shooting until the sun comes up on Saturday morning. The loneliness is hard to cope with and they grow apart. As I am writing this, Denise and I have been married for over 50 years and are still deeply in love, for which I am eternally grateful.

There is a reason they say, "It's show *business,* not show *friend!*" The business has changed over the years. The business is no longer being run by studio heads or movie moguls who knew how to make movies and understood the value of having good people behind the camera.

In the lighting department, it is a young person's business. It was when I came in; the old timers knew it then, and it is still true today. Producers do not like to see old timers on the set. They are afraid they are not going to get their money's worth out of you. It is a hard, physical, dangerous, grueling, demanding, and usually dirty job. We used to joke, "If it were easy, anyone could do it. If it were fun, relatives would be doing it." The movie business thrives on new, young movie makers. They reward new creative thinking. The crew, however, is made up of a mixture of older, more experienced film makers, and younger, more creative and technically advanced film makers. This meld results in better crews with each generation.

I was able to retire with my full pension at age 60. I do not think I could have made it to 65. It turns out I have two compressed disks and a curved spine from 40 years of carrying heavy lights and cables exclusively on my right shoulder. All that being said, there is still no business like show business, and I would do it all again in a heartbeat. But next time, I will carry stuff on my left shoulder once in a while.

I retired from the business with 40 years in. By contract, we can retire at the age of 60 if you have at least 30 years in the business and have at least 60,000 union hours worked. When I reached 60 years old I had 40 years in the business and 80,000 union hours worked. I officially retired on January 1st, 2007. I chose to stay in the union as a retiree with reduced dues and I am still a member. In 2018 I reached the 50-year mark as a member of the union. The office notified me they were going to award my 50-year pin at the next monthly membership meeting. I flew back to Burbank for the meeting. There were five other members at the meeting that I had known for years who were to receive their 50-year pins also. We were awarded a 50-year pin from our Local and a 50-year Membership Award from our International Union. It was a thrill to be able to share this milestone with all of my brothers and sisters at the meeting.

I share here some photos of the union awards and ceremony. I also include photos of my first paycheck in the industry August 1966 and my last one in November 2006. My how those two pieces of paper show the many changes the industry went through from the start through the culmination of my career!

Paul Caven Retirement Photos

**Paul Caven with Patric Abaravich
at Union Retirement Ceremony
(June 2018)**
(Photo from Local's monthly bulletin)

**The International Union 50 Year
Retirement Award**

**Local 728 50 Year
Retirement Pin**

Paul's First Paycheck

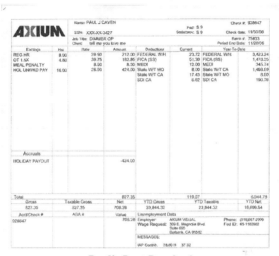

Paul's Last Paycheck

I love when people tell me how much they enjoyed a film I worked on. My contribution may have been small, but it was *not* inconsequential. We all try our best to make a good movie so that when the audience sits down in a theater and the lights go down, we can let ourselves be immersed in the world of make believe. I think Peter Bogdanovich said it best when he wrote:

> "Movies are a language that everybody understands like music for the eyes, and, if you're good, if you're really good, then maybe what you're doing is giving them little tiny pieces of time that they never forget."

Fade to black.

That's a wrap!

POST RETIREMENT LIFE

When I retired, we moved to our farm in rural northwest Missouri. Our new Missouri friends would ask why we moved from California to rural Missouri. I would move up close to them and whisper in their ear, "Three words, witness protection program." We would laugh and then I would explain. Denise's brother, Austin Bonnett, and his wife, Darlene, owned a farm there for years. We would come and visit them on holidays; 4th of July, Thanksgiving or Labor Day. We liked the area. The locals were very friendly. So, I got to thinking, "I'm about to retire, I could do this. I could live here. I could get out of the fast lane." A 40 acre farm came up for sale just down the road from the Bonnett's place, so we bought it.

Denise, Danielle, and I arrived in Missouri for good on April 1st, 2006 (no fooling). We started building our house but I got called back to work in September. I got back to the farm in November and we were able to finally move in on December 15, 2006.

As we got to know people and started becoming familiar with the community, I noticed they had a small theater in the town square of Gallatin, the closest town to our farm. I started asking around and was told that it used to be a movie theater but it closed down in the 1980s. It was currently owned by the local theater group, The Gallatin Theater League. They had been presenting live theater to the community for the last 30 years.

I noticed in the local paper that the Theater League was holding auditions for their spring musical, *Kiss Me Kate*, that Saturday. I decided to go and check it out. The theater people were all great. They were a friendly, fun-loving group. There's no people like show people! But they were a little puzzled as to what I was there for if it was not to audition for a part in their show.

I explained that I was interested in helping with the lighting for the show. Doug Nichols, one of their veteran players said, "Great we have the hardest time trying to talk somebody in to doing that, thanks." Jan Stout, one of the founding members asked, "You mean you don't sing?" I answered, "No, I'm more of a behind the scenes kind a guy." I then went in to a little more detail about my career and how much I would love to help.

Doug said, "Well we would love to let you help, welcome

aboard!" He took me up to the balcony and showed me their lighting control setup. It consisted of 8 regular household dimmer switches that controlled 8 ellipsoidal lights mounted on a pipe about 20 feet from the stage—primitive but effective. I am not criticizing what they did. They did what we all used to do; they did their best with what they had. Actually, it worked fine mechanically. They used it for many years. But lighting-wise, it was all flat, front light. I decided I was going to try to get them a better lighting system.

I put the word out on our union local's email-group (before Facebook) asking if anyone had anything they could donate to help our little hometown community theater. We got some dollar donations but also, one of my friends donated a 125 channel dimmer console. It worked fine, she just wanted a newer model. She could have made money if she sold it, but I was very thankful she decided to donate it to us.

I served on our Local 728 union executive board for six years before I retired so I thought I might still have some pull there. I asked the executive board if they would help us buy some lights and dimmers to use with our newly acquired dimmer console. The union donated $1000.00 with the only stipulation being that it had to go toward buying lighting equipment. I sincerely thanked all my union brothers and sisters for opening up their hearts to our little community theater. I could now add lights and satellite dimmers on stage to be able to light from different angles instead of just from the front. I was now capable of giving them a professional lighting setup and was able to actually do some real lighting for them. It was wonderful to be able to continue to do something I love doing for free for people who really appreciate it.

Later Denise and I both were elected to the theater Board of Directors. The board organized fund raisers and raised enough money to start some work on the interior of the 100-year old theater. Over the next couple of years we extended the stage, we tore out the old seats, sanded down 100 years of gum on the floor, and refinished the floor. We bought refurbished seats, rearranged the lobby and repainted everything.

We have met a lot of wonderful people in the 15 years that we have lived here in beautiful NW Missouri and we have made many good friends here. Over the years I have become involved in our local government. I am currently Vice President of our local School Board. I was recently elected, to our Fire District Board, and have also served on our Township Board. At the time of this writing, I am president of our local Community Betterment Association Board, as well as being involved in the theater. I am busier now in retirement than I ever was before. Actually, I love the fact that I have more time now to be involved with and give back to my community. But, I still find time to sit on my front porch with my feet up and watch my soybeans grow.

Paul's Post-Retirement Selfie

INDEX

287

Made in the USA
Monee, IL
26 March 2022

dad3eacb-612c-4ee7-bf39-95d5611369a9R01